LANGUAGE
AND THE CHILD

Exploring Education

Language
and the Child

M M Lewis

NFER
Publishing
Company
Ltd.

Published by the NFER Publishing Company Ltd.
Book Division, 2 Jennings Buildings, Thames Avenue,
Windsor, Berks., SL4 1QS

Registered Office, The Mere, Upton Park, Slough, Bucks., SL1 2DQ

First Published 1969
Reprinted 1970, 1971, 1973

901225 07 X

Cover Design by Peter Gauld

Printed in Great Britain by
King, Thorne & Stace Ltd., Hove, Sussex, BN3 5JE

Distributed in the USA by Humanities Press Inc.
450 Park Avenue South, New York, NY 10016, USA

Contents

Chapter Notes

Introduction

No MAN is an expert in education—which is perhaps why the school is always a field of criticism and controversy. And one of the centres of fiercest conflict is the teaching of the mother tongue.

This book is an attempt to survey research, observation and thought in their implications for practice in the junior school. But it would be shortsighted to confine ourselves to recent work. The mother tongue has so long a tradition in our schools that what was done in the past throws light on what should be done today, on what changes have become necessary and what remains of value. We have to take a long view and a wide view, not only of research by the linguists and the psychologists, but no less of the thought of the philosophers and the reflections of those skilled in the arts of language—the creative writers.

The book does not pretend to offer new practices. Probably anything that could be suggested is being done by someone somewhere. The intention, instead, is to look at the aims and actual practices of skilled and experienced teachers in the light of two sources of guidance. First, what have research and systematic observation to tell us about the linguistic development of the children by the time they come to us in school? Second, what are the goals towards which we are guiding them—the place of the mother tongue in their lives, at present as children, later as adults?

The book is in three parts. Part I is a survey of the beginnings and early development of children's language and its place in their development. In Part II we describe the various functions of fully-fledged adult language and consider their bearings on the education of the children. Part III discusses the practical implications for the teacher.

The assumption throughout is that a good teacher becomes a better one if he has in mind why he is doing what he does.

PART I

Language and General Development

Chapter One

Influences on Language

IN ONE of his *Notebooks* Samuel Butler says: 'It takes thirty years for a new truth to be recognized; by then it is no longer true'.

This has some force in the history of education. By the time a thought about education has seeped down into general practice, it often lags behind economic, political or ethical changes in society. But the thought and practice of the past are not merely of historical interest. No doubt Dr. Johnson went too far when he said that education is as well known, and has long been as well known, as ever it can be. There are changes in thought about education and new things to be done, but rarely indeed the complete rejection of what was thought and done in the past.

Twenty-five years ago the Norwood Committee had this to say about the place of the mother tongue in education:

> There are three elements essential to a good education . . .
> These elements, which in our view are more than subjects,
> because in one form or another they run through almost every
> activity, intellectual or other, which a school fosters, are:
> training of the body; training of character; training of habits
> of clear thought and the clear expression of thought in the
> English language.[1]

This reflects a growing recognition that the cultivation of the mother tongue must take its place as an equal, side by side with the two time-honoured ideals of English education —physical fitness and character-training. A quarter of a century goes by and the recognition of the importance of the mother tongue is taken a long way further. Now we have this from the Plowden Committee:

> The development of language is central to the educational process.[2]

This is the kind of statement that only too readily invites acceptance and can only too easily become a copy-book maxim for the teacher. But it is in fact different in three important ways from the Norwood statement. First, it emphasizes the importance not simply of language but of its development. Secondly, it sees education also as dynamic, a process. Thirdly, the term 'central' asks us to recognize that the mother tongue not only runs through the whole of education, but that the development of a child depends on the development of his language.

This is a large claim for the mother tongue. If we are not merely to take it for granted, we have to see whether it is really valid in the light of what we know of the development of language; and what this implies for our practice in the junior school.

Four questions follow:

(i) What is a language?

(ii) What are the factors in a child's linguistic development?

(iii) What are the functions of this development in a child's life?

(iv) What are the practical implications?

What is a language?

What is this—a language—that a child progressively grows into, acquires, masters? To know what we should be doing in school, we have to be clear about what lies before the child. But to say what we mean by a language is notoriously difficult. The enormous time and trouble given to the attempt by students of language today has most often led to the conclusion that a language cannot briefly be defined or even described. See, for instance, Strang's *Modern English Structure*, where the whole of the first chapter is devoted to this.[3]

It may well be that the complex nature of a language cannot be fully and accurately described without special technical terms. Fortunately we are not called upon here to attempt a full description. We can confine ourselves to those aspects of language which are of most importance for understanding the development of children. One of the problems is that language is so intimately familiar that we cannot readily stand away from it and view it objectively. For us here the most useful approach is empirical: to look at our mother tongue as we find it in use in adult life and notice what seem to be its essential characteristics; helped, as we can be, by what the linguists have to say.

Language in use, spoken or written, is a form of behaviour; the utterance of words and the response to words, whether by words or in other ways. There is a regularity, a system, in all this; and the study of the systematic nature of language has become one of the main concerns of linguists today. A great deal of time is being given up to studies of the structures of languages—studies which are surveyed in Strang's book mentioned above. The pioneer work of Chomsky on grammatical forms is a special instance of this concern with structures: *Syntactic Structures* (1962).

Chomsky offers us fruitful hypotheses of the ways in which new structures may be 'generated' in the course of acquiring and using a language; we look at the implications of his suggestions later. But he is not primarily interested in the meanings of the structures. In this book our concern must be wider. In the linguistic development of children, structures matter chiefly because of their relationships to their meanings. The language that a child has to acquire is a system, made up of systems of structures and systems of meanings which are systematically related to each other.

We can illustrate this very complex state of affairs by simple examples of familiar words. Take a couple of everyday words with widely different meanings: *walk* and *flower*. We can set down, side by side, six structures involving *walk* with six corresponding structures involving *flower*.

(a) walk	(a) flower
(they) walk	(they) flower
(he) walks	(it) flowers
(riverside) walks	(garden) flowers
walking (stick)	flowering (cherry)
(is) walking	(is) flowering

These are so familiar that we find nothing remarkable in the fact that corresponding structures have corresponding kinds of meanings. As we put it, in the conventional grammatical terms, *walk* or *flower* preceded by *a* is a noun singular; preceded by *they* a verb plural.

Too familiar to be noticed by most people; but it is only if we look at examples of this kind with a fresh approach that we can realize what a child is faced with as he acquires his language. Most children, of course, come to master the complexities of the mother tongue, with little or no awareness of the systematic relations between structures and meanings. But a teacher, at any rate, has to understand what it is that the children have to master: and, more important still, how they achieve this mastery.

In the complex relationships into which the units *walk* and *flower* enter, there are two kinds of structure—syntax and accidence. And although a foreigner at first sight might see only three structures of accidence—*walk, walks, walking* —there are, of course, six of these, since each word occurs as two different parts of speech. Without over-simplification we may put the relationships between accidence, syntax and meaning in this way: syntax determines accidence; meaning determines choice of syntax.

Running through the whole system of a language are its syntactical structures. In English the main obvious regularity of syntax is the order of words, varied according to the intended meaning. There is the old journalists' quip: 'A dog bit a man' is not news, 'A man bit a dog' is.

But syntactical structures are more than arrangements of words; in English, for example, intonation, stress and rhythm are often important factors in syntactical structures, combining to form highly complex systems. A neat example of the place of intonation in a complexity of structure and meaning has been given by A. Lloyd-James.[4] Two people are looking at a picture.

She: Is that Putney Bridge?
He: ....
She: I thought it was.

If she says 'I *thought* it was', his answer has been 'Yes!' If she says 'I thought it *was*', his answer has been 'No!'

For a foreigner all this may be very complicated indeed. Accidence and syntax each presents its own special difficulties. Striking evidence comes from the study of aphasia. Jakobson, for instance, has proposed the terms 'paradigmatic' and 'syntagmatic' to differentiate the diagnosis and the treatment of the impairment of the mastery of accidence and of syntax respectively; and other linguists have adopted these terms to indicate that syntax and accidence may each offer its own challenge to anyone acquiring a language.[5]

The remarkable thing is the speed with which children usually do master the elaborate structural system of the mother tongue. Recent investigations have begun to throw some light on this. Certainly by the age of three many of us have gone a very long way. In a systematic study of about 500 American children from a wide range of homes, Templin found that half the language spoken by the three-year-olds was grammatically correct and that by the age of eight the percentage of correct forms was 75.[6] Even children severely retarded in other respects can often reach a normal level of achievement in language, though of course slowly. In a survey of research Spreen concludes that this may be expected of more than half the children with a non-verbal IQ as low as 50.[7]

What we have to ask is how children achieve this mastery of structures and how this development is related to the expansion and the discrimination of meanings. It is obvious that structure and meaning must influence each other, but it is also clear that the correspondence between a structure and its meaning is not always the same. A particular structure may have different meanings at successive stages of a child's development; or for different children of the same age, even of the same mental age. The word *mother*, for instance, has all this diversity of meanings; we discuss these later (pages 62-3).

Factors in linguistic development

How, then, does this progressive mastery of forms and their meanings occur? The answer seems only too obvious: by imitation. Records show that all children—whether born in London or Paris or Tokyo—utter the same range of sounds in their early months. They cry, or make vocal noises in contentment, or play with sounds; and it can be shown that these are the roots out of which language grows. But it is most important to recognize that if one child comes to speak English and another French, the difference is only partly due to imitation. The systematic observation of children from their earliest months has much to tell us of what happens.

Investigations reported nearly forty years ago by the present writer showed first, that imitation itself changes in the course of a child's development and secondly that it is only one element in a complex process.[8] We can trace during these forty years an increasing confirmation of these conclusions, though their assertion is still necessary. Lenneberg, for instance, enjoins us not to 'forget that imitation actually implies the learning of analytic tools, namely grammatical and phonemic rules'. Chomsky, again, concerned as he is with a child's mastery of structures, reminds us that 'it is a mistake to assume that—past the very earliest stages—much of what the child acquires is acquired by imitation. This could not be true on the level

of sentence formation, since most of what the child hears
is new and most of what he produces, past the very earliest
stages, is new'.[9]

Of course imitation is at work when a French child
learns to say 'table' where an English child says 'table'.
But for the most part this is not simply mimicking sounds
heard. Simple mimicry may certainly happen in early
infancy; but very soon, and more and more, words are
acquired as they are heard and uttered in appropriate
situations; for instance, 'table', 'apple', in the presence of
the things named. While, then, imitation of course plays a
part, it is not the whole story. Observations show that a
child does not mainly imitate the words as labels for things;
'table' for this, 'apple' for that. Soon he is hearing and
responding to words as means of communication. Quite
early, often before the end of the first year, we find a child
responding to such a phrase as 'Have an apple?' by showing
that he wants one and repeating 'Apple'. Or he himself
says 'Table!' and we see that he means something like
'I want to get on the table!' or 'Put me on the table!'

It is clear that throughout all this development, since
imitation is necessary for communication, it is the need to
communicate that keeps a child imitating. We can therefore
go so far as to say that it is communication that chiefly
impels a child to imitate and that he improves his imitations
because of his need to communicate.

When at last a child says, 'Can I have an apple?' and
hears 'Yes, take one from the table', he has moved a long
way from simple imitation. If this can be called imitation
at all, it is that kind of imitation which is learning to use
a means to an end; in this case the use of a particular
verbal structure to bring about a specific result—getting
someone to do something.

To describe, therefore, the acquisition of a language as a
process of imitation is to fall far short of a full account.
Quite early in the course of his development a child, while
he is imitating, is engaged in what is better called 'exploration'; he is still imitative in that he does what he has seen

others do, but he is also exploratory in that he adapts his verbal action according to the present situation, which is both like, and different from, past ones. We must agree with the strictures of Chomsky on the place of imitation: that in responding to speech, most of what the child hears is new and most of what he produces, past the very earliest stages, is new.

For instance, my grand-daughter at the age of three, when asked, 'Where's Humphrey?' answered, pointing, 'That is!' Asked, 'Where's Michael?' answered, 'This is!'

Here we have something much more complex than fixing a verbal label to a person. *That* is not simply a label for Humphrey, nor *this* for Michael.

The child is orientating herself within the situation, responding to different spatial relationships between herself and these other persons and indicating them by different words: *this* and *that*. We are not implying that necessarily the child is aware of these relationships; in fact, we have good grounds for believing that it is possible to act in response to a relationship without being aware of it.[10] Nor are we saying that in such an instance a child is remembering past experiences and deliberately repeating now what he did then. What we can say is that past experiences are enabling him to adapt himself to the present situation. There is a process of transposition—something like transposition in music. While every note is replaced, the pattern of the melody remains. In the *this*, *that*, instance we have just described, it is the pattern of the child's past experience that is transposed to a new situation.

When a child manages to adapt himself in this way to a new situation, we his elders often come in to help him. Even if we don't go as far as telling him how clever he is, at least we show by our manner that we approve; and above all we let him see that we understand him. The strongest encouragement, the main social reinforcement, as some psychologists would term it,[11] comes from the child's realization of his success in communication. From our manner he sees that he is being understood, or is understanding us. All this implies that it is not mainly by imitation, not mainly by learning to put names on things, that a child acquires language, but in the effort to communicate. Communication is the mother of language.

Imitation and exploration

It is important for our understanding of the development of language to recognize that from infancy onwards, and certainly throughout childhood, exploration is one of the main processes. This comes out very clearly in common 'mistakes'.

Mother: Wasn't there an apple on the dish?

Child: Yes, Mummy; I taked it and eated it.

It is unlikely that 'taked' and 'eated' are imitations of words the child has heard, particularly if he has no elder brothers or sisters. Much more probably these forms are the result of a process akin to reasoning by analogy. *I walk, I walked; I talk, I talked; I take, I . . .* A good deal of the time a child will be correct, and receive reinforcement, if he uses the structure 'present tense $+d$ (or t)' to indicate 'pastness'. Where this results in a 'mistake', that is, a form not acceptable in the mother tongue, he will usually be corrected, either directly 'No, not taked, took'; or indirectly, 'I thought that perhaps you took it and ate it'.

What a 'mistake' such as *taked* or *eated* shows very clearly is that a child's mastery of language grows not only by imitation but also by his venturing beyond this. He offers structures—and meanings—that he has never encountered.

The process, we have said, is *akin* to reasoning by analogy. The child is presented with the same sort of problem as he will later come across in an intelligence test:

a : b :: c : ?

for instance,

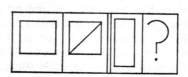

and here: *I walk, I walked; I take* . . .? The form *taked* comes to him as having the same relationship to *take* as *walked* has to *walk*.

We do not imply that the child need be aware of the pattern of relationships, or that he produces this form *taked* by a process of reasoning. What seems much more likely is that his repeated experience of *walked* and *talked* and a multitude of other 'weak verbs' will be enough to establish a tendency for him to indicate the past in this way.

Bartlett—followed by Piaget and others—has helped us to understand this process by showing us that it is a characteristic way in which, in general, past experiences influence subsequent behaviour. A series of experiences establish a *schema;* that is, a pattern of potential behaviour which becomes active in a subsequent situation, alike or different from those previously encountered.[12]

It is much to our purpose here to notice that Bartlett shows that a person may often be unaware of this schematic persistence of the past into the present. It seems reasonable to suppose that this is what happens when a child is acquiring the mother tongue. The unconscious effects of past experience produce a habitual pattern of speech which he uses when he needs to indicate a past event. I once heard a child say: 'I carred home after school'. If a child invents a new verb like this we may well be amused and let it pass. But if he says 'I taked', though he is equally exploratory in making up this form for himself, we are likely to make him realize, in one way or another, that he is making a mistake. How exploratory a child is, how enterprising, will depend very much on how we treat his sallies into the unknown—not only in the beginnings of language but throughout his schooling.

It is by such twin processes of imitation and exploration that the development of language, as of many other skills, takes place. Through both imitation and exploration the forms of a child's language, and their meanings, come nearer and nearer to the language of his social environment. By a constant process of mutual adjustment in

communication with others, he to them and they to him,
his language becomes the current language, the mother
tongue; and the mother tongue becomes his.

The child in communication

The process of mutual adjustment is one aspect of the
unceasing communication between the child and the society
in which he grows up. This communication is, essentially,
the interplay of his tendencies, characteristics, abilities and
temperament with those of other people. At first non-verbal,
communication gives birth to language, which then becomes
its most important medium. All that a child is and does,
alone or with others, has some effect upon the development
of his language.

There is a many-sided, complicated, development in
which a child's life with others influences his thoughts and
his feelings, these influence and are influenced by his
growing language, and language in turn becomes the chief
means of his living with others. These processes, which we
can observe as they occur in infancy, of course continue
throughout his childhood; so that in school the development
of the mother tongue is inseparable from a child's entire
development.

Choosing one thread out of all this, we begin by looking
at the ways in which a child's general development influences
his linguistic development. His growth as a thinking being—
his cognitive development; the emergence of his personality,
individually, socially and ethically—his orectic development; how do these influence his linguistic development? [13]
To this complicated process the child brings his own
potentialities of thought and feeling, influenced as these
constantly are by his life with others.

Cognitive development certainly plays some part from the
very beginning. No doubt—as the research summarized by
Spreen has shown—it is possible for a mentally retarded
child to achieve a considerable command of language, in
utterance and in comprehension. Yet some cognitive

ability is obviously essential. The child must at least be able to recognize the structures of the spoken language and to respond to them in the situations in which they occur.

He may be able to go a long way in using correct forms and in correctly responding to language without giving much attention to the forms themselves or thinking about rules. He may get as far as this through the 'schematic' effects of past experience, as we have described on page 17. But sooner or later, if a child's communication is to become more discriminative and able to embrace a wider range of experience, he will need to bring his mind to bear upon the language he is using and responding to. Usually we see signs of change in the kinds of questions children ask about language. At first they are interested in finding words for the things they see; later, in finding the meanings of the words they come across. In the earlier stages, 'What's this called?' may become a kind of game. Later, a typical question is, 'What does that mean?' [14] At five, my grand-daughter was told that if she continued to misbehave she would make her mother ill. My wife added, 'And then you may have to be looked after by a stranger'. Reply: 'What's a strainer?'— the interest was in the word, not at all in the moral admonition.

It is meaning rather than structure that becomes the most important factor in a child's linguistic development, and it is in semantic rather than structural development that differences among the children become most marked: between those who are more, or less, naturally gifted with potential linguistic ability; between those with impaired and those with normal hearing; between the more and the less intelligent.

Orectic development, again, will influence linguistic development. Even in the earliest stages, differences of temperament may show themselves in children's readiness to communicate; or in their willingness to conform with the ways of their elders. Emotional instability, from one cause or another, may hinder normal progress. Certainly there is some statistical evidence that by the time children are ten years of age the 'better adjusted' are also those who have reached a higher level of linguistic development.[15]

There are, of course, two possibilities here: either a child's emotional difficulties may retard his linguistic development, or retardation in language may adversely affect emotional development. The first of these—the possibility that a child's orectic impairment may adversely affect his language—is supported by a remark of Burt's in discussing the general causes of backwardness: 'Minor psychoneuroses impose a particularly heavy handicap on all intellectual work, dragging the intelligent child down below his possible level of performance and making the dull child seem duller still'.[16] Now since acquisition of a language is to some extent 'intellectual work', we may suppose that it is likely to suffer under emotional stress.

The complementary possibility that language may influence orectic development we discuss later (page 34).

The influence of a linguistic community

While a child's general development may promote or impede his linguistic development, the actual language that comes to be his mother tongue is of course determined by the language of his environment, in a number of ways.

When this diversity of influences is called 'reinforcement', there is a risk of dangerous over-simplification unless we recognize that the relation between a child and his linguistic community is highly complicated. Skinner, for instance, brings the development of language into line with theories of processes of learning by using this—now almost traditional—term 'reinforcement'; verbal behaviour, he says, is 'behaviour reinforced through the medium of other persons'; but then he spends the rest of his large book in elaborating this statement.[17]

For a child a society becomes a linguistic community to the extent that it offers him linguistic experience. To describe this relationship is to spell out the ways in which they must be willing and able to communicate with him; willing to spend time with him, able to use a vocabulary within his range and able to extend it. They must be willing to respond to what he says, encouraging him by letting him see, as far as possible, that they understand him; able to lead him to modify and enlarge his uttered language in accord with the usage of the current mother tongue.

It is through this very elaborate kind of 'reinforcement' that a child's acquisition of the structures and meanings of a language depend upon his relations with his communities and the linguistic experience they provide. Some detailed evidence—if this were needed—comes from the survey by Templin mentioned earlier. She found that the American children she studied were at eight years of age more advanced—in command of structures and in size of vocabulary —than comparable children twenty-five years earlier. She could account for this only by supposing that it is an effect of a general easing of relations between adults and children as well as the richer linguistic experiences afforded by radio and television.

This second kind of linguistic experience is particularly important. A child's growing mastery of meanings—the semantic development of his language—depends on the extent to which he encounters words in a *linguistic* context. In the beginnings of language we cause a child to meet words in relation to actual, concrete situations; what we may call 'situational contexts'. But there comes a time when his first encounter with a word is in a context of words, from which its meaning flows, and not from the direct relation of the word to an actual, concrete, situation.

We have seen one indication of this in the changes in children's questions which show a transition from an interest in the names of things to a concern with the meanings of words. Linguistic contexts come to play a larger and more important part in the child's development. There are even words whose semantic development can hardly, if at all, take place without linguistic contexts. Thus *tall* and *short*, for instance, can be demonstrated in actual situations or in pictures, especially if these are varied enough; but for *mighty* and *weak* we cannot easily manage

without some linguistic contexts, and when we get to
overwhelming and *insignificant*, linguistic contexts are
indispensable.

Just as in the earlier stages it is a child's community that
provides him with situational contexts for language, so
more and more it is his community that provides him with
linguistic contexts. One very important way in which adult
influence offers linguistic experience has been brought out
by Bernstein, in pointing out that the language of a child's
home may do much, or little, to fit him for abstract thinking.
Bernstein compares 'middle-class' with 'working-class'
homes; roughly, professional compared with non-pro-
fessional workers. He suggests that there are important
differences in the range of meanings of the language that
children encounter; middle-class children come to have a
language more apt to be the medium of abstract thinking,
and are therefore better prepared for the language of
school.[18] Certainly we have to recognize that school
introduces a child to a terminology of relatively abstract
meanings, even the primary school; whether in early
mathematics or geography or history—*subtraction, climate,
feudal.* From this there are obvious implications for
children's education in language which we shall need to
consider.

Finally, we must not forget that a child's linguistic
community is not confined to his adult elders. His member-
ship of a community of children—so obviously a powerful
influence on his general development—also makes its own
special contribution to his growing language. This may
begin very early indeed, as a younger child in a family
adopts and adapts the sayings of brothers and sisters.
Later, as the Opies have recorded, while he lives and plays
in a wider community of children, a child may be initiated
into a sub-language not current among his elders; a lingo
of the children themselves.[19]

The special contribution that children make to the
linguistic development of each other is this: words occur
more in the context of a situation than in a context of words.

The words that come into games, or exploration, or trying it on with the grown-ups, or fighting with other groups, are loaded with actuality, emotion and incentive. The words retain and enrich their colour and vitality, while school language may become blanched and vapid. They carry forward into childhood the vigour of infant speech.

At the same time the children maintain, extend and diversify another lively interest of their infancy—they play with language, enjoying a wealth of puns, riddles, rhymes, repartees, traditional rituals.[20] Part of the fun is the cross-talk, the give-and-take instead of the solitary play of infancy. The possibilities of this fascination with words for a child's linguistic education are again obvious.

What are the techniques, the methods?

Because a child's linguistic communities influence both the structures and the meanings of his developing language, and because all this usually turns out so well, it is perhaps natural for a teacher to ask: How is it that a child is brought up in the mother tongue? Can we in the classroom use any of the techniques, the methods that are successful in the home, the street and the playground? The answer is, of course, that unless a child has some special difficulty— deafness, for instance—there is usually no deliberate use of techniques before school and outside school. To get a child to speak, we do not say, 'Speak!' We speak. To get him to understand us, we do not laboriously piece together words and meanings. We speak. We provide him with linguistic experience. He listens while we speak to him and to each other. We ask him and each other questions; we answer his. Rarely do we attempt any direct teaching. The child tries to communicate with us; under the pressure of the need to do this more effectively, he learns to modify and replace his rudimentary cries and noises by our language. We help him in this under the pressure of our own need to communicate with him. Communication is the mother of language.

This remains the basic fact when the child comes to school; a place where adults deliberately set out to carry on his linguistic education. For one of the chief tasks of school has always been, and everywhere still is, to carry forward what the home has begun and to supplement what the home is doing in the linguistic education of every child.

But the techniques cannot simply be carried forward. As every teacher knows, the development of the mother tongue in school is a task full of problems, not to be solved by letting things happen, as they may well do at home. School is a place with special relationships between adults and children, children from different kinds of homes; a place with special aims.

There are traditional methods, some of which have become prescribed techniques. Clearly it might be wasteful, even harmful, to accept them or reject them just because they are old. The teacher who is awake to possibilities and often asks himself, How? finds that he must often ask himself, Why? Our aims become the criteria of our methods.

Language as central to the process of education

To what end? Why be concerned with the linguistic education of a child? We know the pithy reply of the Plowden Report to these questions: 'The development of language is central to the educational process'. This may seem so obvious that it may easily become a catchword empty of meaning. But we here are bound to test its truth; we have to ask what is meant by saying that linguistic *development* is *central* to the *process* of education.

In a simple straightforward sense the statement is a platitude. If by education we mean what goes on in school, then certainly language is necessary for education. All that we have to do is to make sure that a child's language is adequate for the purposes of school.

But the Plowden statement clearly implies much more than this. It speaks of development and process; it sees both language and education as dynamic, as processes of development. And by using the term 'central' it suggests that a child's development *depends* on the development of his language. This is certainly a claim that cannot be taken for granted. It invites questions. Some of the answers come from everyday observation, some from systematic investigation and research. In the next chapters we review these contributions to the answers and see what they have to offer the junior school teacher in clarifying aims and suggesting methods.

Notes

[1] Board of Education: Secondary Schools Examinations Council (1943), p. 19.
[2] Central Advisory Council for Education (England) (1967), p. 66.
[3] The linguists struggle with description. Strang quotes Hockett, who finds it necessary to use these terms: duality, productivity, arbitrariness, interchangeability, specialization, displacement, cultural transmission.
[4] Lloyd-James (1935), p. 95.
[5] A discussion of Jakobson's views and their implications is reported in Osgood and Miron (1963), pp. 68-71.
[6] Templin (1957), p. 96; summarized in Lewis (1963), p. 107.
[7] Spreen (1965), p. 485. Lenneberg (1964a), p. 46, summarizing his own and others' work, says: 'Children whose IQ is 50 at age twelve, and about 30 at age twenty, are completely in possession of language, though their articulation may be poor and an occasional grammatical mistake may occur'.
[8] Lewis [(1951). 1st ed. 1936], ch. 6; Lewis (1963), pp. 22-6.
[9] Lenneberg (1964b), p. 122; Chomsky (1964), p. 37.
[10] Lewis (1963), pp. 41-2, particularly the quotation from G. F. Stout
[11] See p. 25 and chapter note 17 (below).
[12] Lewis (1963), p. 40; and also references to *schema* in the Index there.
[13] *Orectic* is a convenient word to cover the emotional, social and ethical aspects of personality. 'Orexis: the conative and affective aspects of experience—impulse, attitude, desire, emotion'. J. Drever, *Dictionary of Psychology*, 1952. Harmondsworth: Penguin.
[14] For an instance of both kinds of question in a child's third year, see Lewis (1963), p. 95.
[15] Sampson (1964), p. 149; Rushton (1966), p. 180.
[16] Burt (1937), p. 554.
[17] Skinner (1957), p. 14. The doubts of many workers that social linguistic relationships can be adequately termed 'reinforcement' have been voiced by Chomsky in a scathing review of Skinner's book [Chomsky (1959)].
[18] Bernstein (1958), pp. 161-4; (1960), p. 179; (1964), pp. 56-8. For a critical summary, see Lawton (1968), ch. 5.
[19] Opie and Opie (1959), ch. 1.
[20] Opie and Opie (1959), ch. 5.

Chapter Two

Functions of Language

IN THINKING about anything as ancient as education in language, it is impossible to see clearly where we stand today unless we look back at the past. We need perspective. What changes have recent thought and investigation to suggest; what remains unchanged? The Norwood Report, for instance, gives indications of what was considered worthy of special emphasis twenty-five years ago. It implies two main functions of language for a child: the expression of thought and training in habits of clear thought.

What strikes us most forcibly about this is that it is so restricted. We would say today that the importance of the mother tongue for a child goes far beyond expression, far beyond communication—that it is the most powerful means of educating him. We would say that language not only communicates thought but also emotions, desires, intentions and much else. More exactly, language in communication symbolizes and evokes both cognitive and orectic behaviour.

But language is not only used in communication with others. Often we use language privately, speaking to ourselves or writing for our own benefit. And when we look at these functions of language for an individual himself, we see that they go far beyond what the Norwood Report suggests.

First, language not only serves the purposes of 'clear thought'. It is true that alone, not in communication with anyone, we use language for recalling what has happened; for recording for the future; for solving problems; for anticipating and planning. Any of this may be overt, in writing or in speaking to ourselves; or it may be covert, within ourselves, imagined language, 'inner language'. These are among the ways in which language may not only help to achieve habits of clear thought but may also serve a wide range of cognitive tasks, over the whole of our intellectual life.

But no less may language serve the needs of our orectic life—our individuality as persons; our attitudes, intentions and purposes. Language within ourselves may help in forming our pictures of ourselves as we are and as we may become; may help us in coming to terms with our emotions and desires, and help to organize, control and direct these; may help in defining our purposes, and forming and clarifying our judgements of right and wrong and in promoting our awareness of our ethical conduct.

Much of this is of course beyond the life of a child in the junior school; but however imperfect his language may be, the beginnings of all these functions are there. It is only by recognizing their rudiments, in their range and diversity, that we can hope to have a full view of the place of the mother tongue in the junior school. When we come to discuss the practical implications of this, we shall have to consider what a teacher can do to help the children to make good use of their private language.

Having said this, it becomes evident that there is no line of separation between the communicative and the private functions of language. Much of our personal language, whether overt or inner, must begin as communication. It is worth noticing that Piaget, who in his early work so strongly maintained that egocentric language in infancy has a life of its own, relatively independent of communication, now sees the force of Vigotsky's view that it has its sources in social language, in communication with others.[1]

On the other hand, private language, whether overt or inner, is often used in preparation for communication. We go over in our minds what we are going to say, or we make notes. While therefore it is essential for our work as teachers to recognize that language has both private and communicative functions, we have still to bear in mind that in our everyday experience they are closely inter-related.

For the sake of clarity in our survey here, we discuss them separately; but while we do so we shall need to take account of their mutual influences.

1. The functions of language in communication

As teachers we are concerned with the different functions of communication because they demand somewhat different kinds of language, with corresponding differences in our aims and our methods in school. But our concern with communication is also our concern with private language. While we are developing a child's linguistic education through communication, we are at the same time influencing the nature and functions of his private language.

Manipulative and Declarative Functions

There is one broad distinction, the beginnings of which are already to be seen in infancy and which continues throughout life in communicative language, whether spoken or written. There are two different functions which can be most easily distinguished as they occur in their rudimentary forms. Take, for example, two recorded instances of the use of 'mama' by the same child in his tenth month.[2]

(a) Confined in his 'play-pen' he tries in vain to reach his ball. He says 'mamama' urgently. When his mother comes and gives him the ball, his word has had a *manipulative* effect.

(b) He says 'mammam' in a very contented tone, while lying in his mother's lap and looking up at her. When she smiles and perhaps speaks to him, his word is having a *declarative* effect.

The manipulative effect is to cause the child's mother to do something for him, to perform some task. The declarative effect is to establish rapport between the child and his mother. Only in a very crude sense can the child be said to utter the 'same' word 'mama' on both occasions. There are linguistic differences corresponding to the different circumstances—differences in speed, stress, intonation, pausing and manner of repetition.

To us these differences convey different meanings. For the child himself, how far the two functions are, at this stage, intentional we cannot say. Certainly as time goes on they become so. In adult life we see them as clear differences in the intention of a speaker and in the responses of a listener. Each function now covers a wide span of experience and behaviour.

The manipulative function comes to include all those uses of language which are primarily intended to cause another person to engage in some action, 'to do something', whether now or later. Instructions, information, commands, requests, advice—all these are forms of manipulative communication. They can all be said to be intended to evoke 'doing something', especially when we remember that doing includes saying; so that one very important manipulative function occurs in conversation between people. Skinner, in his elaborate analysis of the working of language, calls this interchange 'intra-verbal behaviour'—the effects of words upon words. He points out that some linguists have had difficulty in fitting conversation into a definition of language, as behaviour that evokes behaviour, because they have been unwilling to recognize that language is itself behaviour.[3]

The declarative function comes to include all those uses of language where the primary intention is to induce communion between speaker and listener, writer and reader. It is seen most clearly in its simplest form, in the ordinary everyday exchange of greetings, where its function is what the anthropologist Malinowski christened 'phatic communion': 'a type of speech in which ties of union are created by a mere exchange of words'.[4] 'Good morning!' 'How do you do?' 'Fine day!'—we are not asking anyone to do anything; we are not even telling him anything; we are only getting into touch, into communion, with him. Certainly this is no less important a use of language than the manipulative function. We can observe the development of the declarative function from its rudiments in infancy to the part it plays in the most complex forms of imaginative literature.

What all this brings home to us is that we cannot speak of *the* function of language; the manipulative and the declarative functions must be clearly distinguished— although they are often found together.

Structure and Function

The two functions must be distinguished if we are to give each its necessary place in a child's education in language. But often enough, in adult language as in infancy, what is outwardly the 'same' verbal structure—word, phrase or sentence—may, on different occasions, have either a manipulative or a declarative function. The semantic differences may then be so profound as to make two different linguistic symbols of the 'same' verbal structure.

Question: What is the price of this house?

Answer: Ten thousand.

Compare this with Wordsworth's

> Ten thousand saw I at a glance
> Tossing their heads in sprightly dance.

It is not enough to say that *ten thousand* has two different functions here; there are two substantially different meanings, which may be present not only in communication but also in inner language.

These two functions are often distinguished by using the terms first made current by Ogden and Richards now more than forty years ago. In their well-known discussion they made a contrast between the emotive and the symbolic or referential uses of language; in the emotive use the speaker expresses and evokes feeling, in the referential use he refers and draws attention to a situation.[5] This is not the essential distinction here. It certainly would not be true to say that the house-agent's *ten thousand* is only referential while Wordsworth's is only emotive. What the house-agent says is something more than a statement of so many pounds. *He* hopes; *we* may be surprised or annoyed. While what he says is mainly referential, it is also emotive.

By contrast, Wordsworth's *ten thousand*, while it certainly has an emotive function—symbolizing the 'glee' and 'pleasure' he mentions in the poem—has also a referential function. It refers us to the picture of a multitude of daffodils.

The essential difference in the two functions of *ten thousand* here is in the effect—actual or potential or intended—upon the listener. The mention of the price of the house is manipulative, it suggests an action to the listener, payment. The function of Wordsworth's phrase is quite different in its possible or actual effect on the reader. It suggests no action. It establishes or seeks to establish rapport with the reader, but it is none the less referential.

These distinctive functions, which are primarily functions in communication, are carried over into private language; so that when I think of *ten thousand* as the price of a house, part of its meaning is manipulative; when I think of it in the context of the daffodils part of its meaning is declarative.

These are obvious distinctions which may, however, be lost if we speak of 'the' meaning of a word or phrase, instead of seeing the word in relation to its relevant situation, to its linguistic context and to its function. In childhood there are already the rudiments of these distinctions; different meanings of the 'same word'. Gradually, under the influence of home and school, the meanings come nearer to, and finally to correspond to, the ranges of meaning in the current mother tongue; we look at these in the next chapter.

2. Private language

A great deal of speech in infancy is not communication with another person. While he is going about his everyday business, and particularly while he is playing, a child will often be heard talking to himself. With many children this is a regular thing after the age of two.

Sometimes this self-addressed speech seems to be no more than a concern with, a pleasure in, the words themselves—a persistence and development of the babbling of early infancy. Now the child plays with words and phrases as formerly he played with sounds. R. H. Weir has recently made an exceptionally careful record and analysis of the private talk of her two-and-a-half year-old son, night after night, before sleep; a study highly illuminating for our understanding of private language. She shows that in the course of his self-addressed speech the child was practising the mastery of verbal structures of the mother tongue.[6]

Private speech has another important value in a child's development. What he says to himself may have an immediate bearing on what he is doing at the time. He may describe what he is doing, but only for his own benefit. He may ask questions of himself and find answers not in words but in action.

Examples from the record of a boy in the earlier part of his third year are:

2;2 yrs. Looking through a picture-book, he finds the picture of a teddy bear. Shuts the book and says: *Ever can teddy bear be?* He repeats all this many times.

2;3 yrs. Playing the game of hiding a pencil in a book: *Ever can you be, little pencil?*

2;4 yrs. Looking for his toy, 'Billy-boy'; *Billy-boy, where Garkie put it? Where is it?*

2;4 yrs. Playing with his train, looking for the string: *Where's the string?*[7]

This is the kind of speech that Piaget called egocentric, a term which unfortunately gave rise to a good deal of confusion—as McCarthy has shown in her summary of subsequent work.[8] Egocentric could mean spoken *to* oneself, or spoken *about* oneself; Piaget, it is clear from the context, means the former. He emphasizes its chief function: 'it serves to accompany, reinforce or supplant action'.[9] My own observations suggested that this self-addressed speech is more than an accompaniment to action; that it is part of the action, which is thus both non-linguistic and linguistic. The words are a means by which a child is helped to direct his attention, to regulate what he is doing, to 'think aloud'.[10] Subsequently Vigotsky named this kind of speech 'synpractic'; indicating not only that it accompanies action, but also emphasizing its functions in contributing to and promoting activity—the mental and physical action with which it is intimately interwoven. 'It serves', he says, 'mental orientation, conscious understanding; it helps in overcoming difficulties'.[11]

Synpractic speech is evidently of great importance in a child's linguistic and general development. While it may have the appearance of communication, it would be misleading to call it the communication of the child with himself. There is certainly some inner speech by which a child does communicate with himself; the language which precedes or follows thought or feeling or physical action; when, for instance, he tells himself what has happened or what is going to happen in the future. But synpractic language is different. It is interwoven with thought, feeling or action, as the verbal element in whatever the child is engaged in at the moment. For instance, the boy's 'Where's the string?' is an integral part of the action of looking for the string. One can see that, as Vigotsky suggests, this self-addressed speech may then be internalized and so become a means by which a child may regulate and organize his inner cognitive and orectic behaviour.[12]

3. Cognitive and orectic influences of language

In the last chapter we noticed the possible influences of cognitive and orectic development on the development of language. We saw that cognitive processes such as conceptual thinking, remembering and reasoning may affect the development of language; and also that it may be influenced by orectic characteristics such as temperament and emotional stability. Now we have to look at possible effects in the other direction: the influences of language upon a child's cognitive and orectic development.

Language as an Influence in Cognitive Development

There is no doubt that language may enter into and influence every kind of cognitive process—whether this be perceiving, conceptual thinking, remembering, planning or reasoning. This has long been recognized; to the extent even of identifying thought with language. By Plato's time it was possible to put this forward as a provocative statement in an argument; he makes Socrates say: 'When the mind is thinking, it is talking to itself'. The modern counterpart of this is the more cautious remark by Bertrand Russell: 'Almost all higher intellectual activity is a matter of words to the nearly total exclusion of everything else'.[13]

Today, a balanced view suggests that probably all cognitive processes may, up to a point, take place independently of language; but that for most of us, cognitive development has been influenced by language, both in communication and privately within ourselves. The evidence is that as cognitive processes become more complex and more abstracted from immediate sensory experience, language plays an increasingly important part; and that there may be a level of 'higher intellectual activity' at which language is indispensable.

On the other hand, there is some evidence that the misuse of language may impair the development, and hinder the exercise, of cognitive processes.[14] We shall need to look at the practical implications of this many-sided relationship in some detail later.

Language as an Influence in Orectic Development

The place of language in orectic development and its influence on orectic processes are less clear. But there is good reason to believe that the account that we have just given of the influences of language on cognition has its parallels in orectic life.[15]

Central to a child's orectic development is the emergence of his personality—his personal traits as an individual; and his character, his ethical development. On the place of language in all this, a guiding clue has been given us by

Freud. Describing the emergence of the ego, the pattern of personal characteristics; and of the super-ego, the pattern of ethical judgements and attitudes, he finds the chief influence to be 'the voice of the father'.[16] It is clear from the context of Freud's exposition that he means that in this personal development the influence of a child's elders is brought to bear on him through linguistic communication.

We can see the force of this. The pattern of traits that go to make up a personality have their primary source, no doubt, in inborn temperament. But as a child grows up amongst other people, it is in the give-and-take of everyday social life that his primary characteristics develop into more or less permanent traits. As others give names to these traits, language helps the child himself to become more readily aware of them. This function of language has been emphasized by G. H. Mead: 'The importance of communication lies in the fact that it provides a form of behaviour in which the individual may become an object to himself'.[17] He is suggesting that just as language helps a child to become more clearly aware of objects in the world around him—indeed, to establish them for him as objects—so language becomes a means of self-awareness, helping a child to look at and see himself.

As he grows up he accumulates names, for himself and for his traits. He is Tom Jones, Tommy, brother, son, cousin, nephew, friend, schoolboy, champion swimmer. He is said to be kind, cheeky, lazy, slow, careless. And as these names come to him from without, they evoke responses in him, sometimes of conformity, sometimes of rejection. Sooner or later they are incorporated into his private inner language, colouring his vision of himself and influencing the direction of his further development.

Inseparable from this development of his personality is his *ethical development*, throughout which, as Freud reminds us, communication is again a powerful influence. The beginnings are usually to be seen within the first year. As soon as a child is mobile enough to wander beyond reach of his mother's hand, her only effective means of guiding and guarding him at a distance is the word *No!* Samuel Butler has said that a tool is often only a means of lengthening one's arm. The word *No!* is a mother's most useful linguistic instrument.

A typical instance comes from the record of a child in his tenth month:

> He has seized a piece of newspaper which he is about to put into his mouth. I say *No!* in a loud voice. Immediately he stops the movement of his hand and looks towards me. He keeps his eye steadily on me for a minute or so, then turns back to continue the movement of the paper towards his mouth. I say *No!* again. Again he turns towards me and stops the movement of his hand.[18]

As time goes on we can often witness a striking development. A child, obviously about to do something that is forbidden, says *No!* and desists. The word is on its way to becoming a means by which the child can control his own behaviour. Soon it is likely to be incorporated in his inner language, so that he carries within himself a verbal symbol of some prohibition of his society. It is an instance of the process by which, as Vigotsky suggests, a word which begins in communication becomes internalized. The prohibition the child may either accept or reject, and he can do so the more readily now that it has a verbal form that he can attend to, think about.

Again, from the ranks of the experimental psychologists, Skinner, in an approach as different as possible from that of Freud, nevertheless accepts his view of the function of inner language in ethical life. 'The Freudian super-ego . . . the conscience, is essentially verbal. It is the still, small *voice*'.[19] We can see that one element in the development of conscience, from the beginning, is certainly direct precept, the *Yes!* and the *No!* which continue throughout life in the elaborate forms of codes of conduct, a body of prohibitions and sanctions.

But direct precept is not the only form of linguistic influence upon ethical attitudes and conduct. Children are influenced by the expression of approval or disapproval addressed to others in their hearing; and, no less, by attitudes expressed about the conduct of people not actually present. And this is where stories heard, read, pictured, play their part; influences all the more powerful precisely because the child is not directly addressed.

We get insight into this by noticing what happens to children whose language development is unfortunately impaired.

Here is Jane, eleven years old. Severely deaf, she wears a hearing-aid but has to rely upon lip-reading. At breakfast she and Mary, her sister with normal hearing, pick up a great deal from what Mother and Father say to each other. This morning they have been talking about John. Jane, watching her mother's lips, catches this intriguing sentence: 'I'm inclined to think that John is right'.

Now Jane is an intelligent girl, with a good vocabulary for her age and her degree of deafness. She 'knows the meaning' of *right*; it names one side of her body and the hand she uses in writing and sewing. As it happens, she also 'knows the meaning' of *inclined*; some days ago in school her teacher drew a sloping line on the blackboard and below it the word *inclined*.

What does Jane make of her mother's remark?

What Jane gets in so garbled a form is what children with normal hearing receive with ease, day in and day out. And this is one of the chief ways in which they are influenced by adult attitudes and codes of conduct. This is not to say that they will always conform to these ethical codes and attitudes; only that the linguistic expression of them helps a child to be more readily aware of them, more readily able to carry them in mind, and so to be clearer about what he is accepting or rejecting. It is certainly difficult to over-estimate the importance of language in ethical development, whether directly by way of precept, or indirectly.

On the *emotional* aspects of orectic development, language has no less powerful influences. Language becomes a stimulus evoking emotions; an influence on the stability of their organization; and a means by which a child comes to exercise control over them. We can look briefly at these three effects of language.

Language as a stimulus: from a very early age language becomes a stimulus for the arousal of emotions, supplementing and largely replacing non-linguistic stimuli. Emotions which at first were aroused by physical conditions, including the acts of others, now are evoked by words.

The Opies tell us that children still chant

> Sticks and stones may break my bones
> But names will never hurt me.[20]

But most of us remember that 'names' hurt us more deeply and enduringly than sticks. Certainly in adult life our emotions are aroused less often by what we experience at first-hand than by words addressed to us, or by what we hear or read about. Language becomes a powerful means of stimulating emotions.

Children in the junior school are moving in this direction, and their orectic education consists very largely in fostering this development. In school—whether we realize it or not—we are constantly influencing the children to have the 'right feelings'; that is, the emotions acceptable, approved, by us their society. In their social education, the right feelings towards people: we incite the children to be angry at reports of cruelty; we encourage them to be sympathetic, compassionate towards the unfortunate. In their aesthetic education we try to influence their feelings towards what is 'beautiful' or 'ugly' in the world of nature and of art. And, as we have seen, in their ethical education we attempt to develop the 'right' sentiments and attitudes: to admire honesty, courage, self-sacrifice; to despise lying, cowardice. We do this not so much by direct injunctions, as indirectly by the communication of our own attitudes, largely through language; and also by bringing them a wealth of vicarious experience through the spoken and the written word.

Language and Emotional Organization

A second effect of language is its influence on the organization of emotions.

What we mean by the organization of emotions is best seen when we speak of 'maladjusted' children. We have in mind not only that they are not well adjusted in their relationships with other people; at the same time we associate these defective relationships with disorganization within themselves. We say that they are unstable—unpredictable and inconsistent in the kind and strength of their emotions. We say that they are uncontrolled—that they do not inhibit the expression of their emotions to the extent that we are accustomed to expect of children of their age. Now when we make these judgements, our criteria are socially determined; they are the criteria current in a social group, smaller or larger. There are even said to be ethnic differences: as, for instance, the contrasts commonly made between Italians and Englishmen; for instance, a man thought to be unduly reserved in Italy might pass muster in England. Hamlet was told it was well to send a madman to England; 'Twill not be seen in him there; there the men are as mad as he'.

Since the criteria are, in a measure, socially determined, language may obviously play an important part in the organization of a child's emotional life. Luria and other Russian workers have emphasized the *regulatory* function of language.[21] They adduce systematic observations to show that as children normally learn, through communication, to subordinate their behaviour to instructions, ultimately some of this regulatory function is taken over by inner language. This then plays a part in regulating and organizing not only physical behaviour but also 'thought and volitional action'.

We need hardly add that children remain vastly different from each other in their emotional make-up, because of inborn temperament and the extent to which they respond individually to the influences of others. Powerful among these influences is language, through which a child's community plays its part in his individual emotional development.

Language and Social Development

The most obvious orectic influence of language is on a child's social development.

From a very early moment indeed in infancy he finds his place in the family by what is said to him, said in response to him, said about him. Here again language replaces non-linguistic behaviour. The beginnings are seen as soon as someone answers an infant's cry, not only by doing something but by saying something. Mother says, as she gets his milk ready, 'Coming, Baby!' The time comes when these words are sufficient to soothe the crying child, when he makes responsive sounds expressive of satisfaction even before he sees the milk.

From this early time onwards, vocal interchange becomes more and more an important kind of relationship with others. There is a verbal social relationship, which at first supplements and then supersedes some of the physical relationships. This communication within the family has features of its own. Sometimes there is a special little vocabulary and special intonations—a special 'register', as linguists now call the language which is characteristic of a particular social situation.[22] This language reflects and promotes the intimacies of family life, so that the interchange of words becomes one of the main ways of living together. Through the mother tongue, a somewhat precarious equilibrium, sensitive to delicate pressures, is established between the child and father and mother, sisters and brothers.

As he enters the wider community of his contemporaries beyond his home, and his social development becomes more complex, in this again language has a basic function. His incorporation into the social life of a group of children is often at the same time the acquisition of another esoteric sub-language, as the Opies have shown us with a wealth of detailed observations.[23] Again a social community becomes also a linguistic community; for a child to participate in the sub-language of the group is to identify himself with the group. While doing what the group expects him to do, he has the sense of having some say in what is being done. The importance of this for a child's social development is twofold.

First, he has to learn to come to terms with his contemporaries on a basis of *mutuality* rather than of his usual subordination to elders, including—if he is a younger child—brothers and sisters. Observations by Piaget and Susan Isaacs show that this growth of mutuality is a stage in a child's development on his way to becoming a mature adult person, able to take his place in life with other mature persons.[24]

The sub-language can also be—and should be—a stage in a child's linguistic development. The importance of this special enlargement of his linguistic experience must not be minimized. The earthiness of the sub-language, including its scatology, can be an extension of language, making the growing child ultimately more fit—not less fit—to enter the widest linguistic community of all: the community in which it is the special task of the school to initiate him. This is the linguistic community which embraces the past as well as the present. For us in the western world it extends at least from classical literature and the Bible to the recorded spoken word and the newspaper of today.

If a child is ultimately to become a member of this widest linguistic community he needs a corresponding width of linguistic experience. This is where every kind of sub-language has a contribution to make. The lingo recorded by the Opies—with its puns, its slang, its schoolboy obscenities—may seem a far cry from 'literature'; but it leads on to a more natural, a more mature, approach to Shakespeare, for instance, than the special notes at the back of the book; or whispered gigglings in class; or, worst of all, bowdlerization.

This suggests a degree of tolerance of the freer language of the young than would perhaps be acceptable by all teachers. But already it is on the way to acceptance by some, who are finding the concept of 'register' helpful here;

that different kinds of communication demand corresponding structural and semantic differences in speech and in writing.

Since such a differentiation of register according to situation, purpose and the linguistic community goes far in ordinary everyday life, for the school the question is whether it can be accepted as a positive goal in education. We consider this in our discussion of the basic principles of practice in Chapter 5.

4. The concurrence and diversity of functions

Before we leave the description of the functions of language, one thing more must be said. These various functions that, for convenience and clarity, we have considered separately, often occur together, if not simultaneously.

We have already suggested that language in communication and private individual language are closely inter-related. Language is commonly also both declarative and manipulative, though one of these functions usually predominates. If a poem, which is predominantly declarative, sooner or later influences the behaviour of listener or reader, this is a manipulative effect; even though there may not have been a manipulative intention by the poet. On the other hand, a technical treatise, primarily manipulative, intended as a guide to operative skills, may have a declarative effect on the reader; his admiration, for instance, of the skill and clarity of the presentation.

Again, language—whether communicative or private—is rarely, if ever, purely cognitive or orectic in function; for our behaviour is rarely, if ever, simply one or the other. When we are engaged in a mainly cognitive task, feelings and desires may enter any or all of its aspects and phases: perceiving, recalling, problem-solving, planning. The course of the task may produce pleasure or discomfort, frustration or satisfaction, and the language in which the task is presented or presents itself may evoke any of these orectic effects.

On the other hand, orectic behaviour and attitudes commonly, if not always, involve cognitive processes. In our personal, ethical, emotional and social attitudes and behaviour we obviously often need to perceive, recall, reason and plan. Here again language, whether social or private, may have an influence. In communication with others, or within ourselves, language which is primarily orectic may still evoke any of these cognitive processes.

For the teacher, the possible concurrence of functions always raises one practical question, What is the dominant intention and what are its effects? If language is to be central to the process of education, as the Plowden Report suggests, this is not to be achieved by ignoring the diversity of the functions of language. On the contrary, the teacher must constantly keep in mind that the different functions make correspondingly different demands on him and on the children.

In their everyday life the children have frequent experience of the concurrence of functions, in communication and in their private language. For their continued development in language they need to become more clearly aware of the diversity of functions—where communication is manipulative, where declarative, where more referential, where more emotive. From a very early moment, as we have seen, their own speech and their responses will vary. Some awareness of the differences will emerge, merely from their repeated experience. It becomes the task of the school in the cultivation of the mother tongue to sharpen this awareness in the children's reading and writing, listening and speaking. For the sensitivity of their responses and of their own uses of words will depend, as they grow up, on this awareness.

This cannot be hurried; there is a danger—as in so much else in education—of a forced precocious growth. It is, rather, something to be nurtured over the years.

In this the teacher in the junior school has a full part to play, requiring his discretion and his skill. He must have a clear idea of what it is that he is helping to produce. In Part II, therefore, we look at the kinds of communication and of private language, as they occur in adult life, in order to distinguish the various functions of each, as a guide to our goals in the education of the children. The practical problems that arise in school we then consider in Part III.

Notes

[1] Piaget (1923), p. 55; Vigotsky (1962), pp. 17-9.
[2] Lewis (1963), p. 61.
[3] Skinner (1957), p. 128.
[4] Malinowski (1923), p. 315.
[5] Ogden and Richards (1949), p. 10 and throughout the book.
[6] Weir (1963), p. 108.
[7] Lewis (1963), p. 92.
[8] McCarthy (1954).
[9] Piaget (1923), p. 27.
[10] Lewis (1963), pp. 92, 236.
[11] Vigotsky (1962), p. 133.
[12] Vigotsky (1962), p. 19.
[13] Russell (1921), p. 29. A summary of the history of this discussion is in Lewis (1947), pp. 84-92.
[14] Evidence is summarized in Lewis (1963), chs. 3, 5, 7, 10; and in Lunzer and Morris (1968), vol. 2, particularly ch. 5. The special effects of deafness in children are illuminating; see Furth (1966) and Lewis (1968).
[15] Lewis (1963), chs. 4, 8, 11, and Lunzer and Morris (1968), vol. 2, pp. 164-8.
[16] Freud (1927), p. 29.
[17] Mead (1934), p. 138.
[18] Lewis (1963), p. 43.
[19] Skinner (1957), p. 444. Freud's views are so often said to be subjective that it is particularly striking to find this approach from Skinner who above all aims at objective evidence.
[20] Opie and Opie (1959), p. 160.
[21] Luria (1959) and Luria (1961).
[22] Strang (1962), p. 19: 'the distinctive forms of language adopted in relation to particular social roles'.
[23] Opie and Opie (1959), throughout.
[24] Lewis (1963), pp. 214, 221-2.

PART II

Growing Up in a Literate World

Chapter Three

The Child Encountering Language

SO FAR we have been speaking about the part language plays in a child's life; how it develops and what its functions are. Now we go on to ask ourselves: What are his needs in his continued linguistic education? Some are immediate—his needs while he is still with us in the junior school; then there are the needs of his later schooling, his secondary education and, finally, his needs in adult life. While these needs shade imperceptibly into each other, a teacher has to keep them distinct in his mind so as to be clear about what he is trying to do in school.

A child has three kinds of experience of language. He encounters it when others are communicating with him, when he is communicating with others, and in his own private uses. Already in childhood, each of these can be informal or more formal.

Informal communication with and from a child is his everyday conversation at home, in the street, in school, in the playground—all developing out of his early rudimentary interchanges with his mother. The informal private language of his childhood is a continuation and development of the beginnings of self-addressed speech that we have described in Chapter 2.

As a child grows up amongst adults, he encounters the more formal uses of language. These come to him as he listens to stories and later learns to read them for himself; when in communication with others he begins to write; when in his private language he uses writing as a help to what he is doing, thinking and feeling. These can be called the more literate uses of language since they are influenced by, and even depend upon, the written word. A child today lives in a literate world long before he comes to school. Even the earliest stories he listens to, if they have not actually been written, are likely to have been influenced in form and style by what the teller has read. Literate language today is part of every child's linguistic experiences; in the books he reads, in the radio and television he listens to, and in his own writing, certainly when it is for others and even when it is for himself.

A child therefore comes to us in the junior school both with a long history of informal language and with the beginnings of formal language. But although from infancy he has been bathed in a sea of language, it is for us to ensure that he does not flounder about aimlessly. We work blindly unless we have some idea of the direction in which we should be moving.

Discussions with teachers show that the teaching of English often suffers from a lack of order and direction. Where is guidance to come from? We can be helped by looking back as well as forward. Much can be learnt from what we know of children's development as we have outlined it in the previous chapters. To help children to move forward, we must be guided by what we know of the uses of language, as we see them in adult life. The fully-fledged forms must have their influence on every stage of a child's education. We have to keep them in mind; not with the aim of achieving them while he is still a child, but so that we have before us the goals, distant though they may be, towards which we should be helping him to move.

Everyday communication in adult life

Daily conversation is written as well as spoken. The interchange which arises from and promotes the business of living together is not only face to face or by telephone; it also needs the post office. If, as some are now thinking, the written word is to be overtaken and replaced by speech and the seen image, that day is not yet.

In conversation, whether spoken or written, we have in more highly developed forms the declarative and manipulative functions the rudiments of which we have seen in infancy. Everyday conversation is declarative when it is the 'phatic communion' described by Malinowski, the interchange which is intended to produce rapport, communion with another person: 'Good morning', 'How do you do?' 'Please', 'Thank you'. Even in adult life this declarative speech is hardly more informative than the declarative noises made by a baby. Oscar Wilde once defined a bore as a man who, when you ask him 'How are you?', *tells* you. Written as well as spoken conversation can be declarative; a personal letter is often no more than hailing someone at a distance, a way of getting in touch with him, rather than telling him anything.

Oscar Wilde's remark draws a boundary line round the limits of declarative language. As soon as a person asks a question which requires an informative answer, we are getting beyond the bounds of purely declarative language. While therefore it is important to recognize the declarative element in most everyday language, it is equally important to notice what happens when this becomes informative. I tell someone what has happened or what may happen; or I explain something to him, tell him how a process is to be carried out; or I try to set out a sequence of ideas. These kinds of narrative or expository communication may be partly declarative, but their main function is manipulative, in that they set the listener to work, mentally or physically; getting him to start a course of thinking or carry out a series of physical acts; or both.

Everyday style, spoken and written

Because everyday spoken conversation, declarative or manipulative or both, has its own colloquial register—such things as the proper forms of address, the choice of words and the use of idioms—it offers a problem to a child learning to write and to his teacher. Are the colloquial forms of everyday speech to be carried over into everyday writing? [1]

Here we come across an interesting historical development. Today the language of personal letters is probably nearer the spoken word than ever before. If we go back and look at letters written more than two centuries ago, their English suggests not that people were speaking to each other as formally as that, but rather that the letters are in the style and register of written language. Today the gap is narrower; we write our letters rather as we speak. But how far are we to go in this? Can a teacher tolerate such colloquialisms as 'Who did you give my book to?'; 'I told him it was me'; 'Between you and I'? Sir Ernest Gowers in his campaign for plain English tells us that all these three are within the usage of distinguished writers; but even he is uneasy at recommending us to use them in our own writing.

As teachers we probably have to be less conservative. Unless we have the courage to be tolerant of colloquialisms we are in danger of arousing the resistance which is always latent in some children—resistance to our attempts at their linguistic education, resistance to our rules as pedantic, unreal and 'teachery'. They may perforce acquiesce while in the classroom; but we hope for more lasting effects of our work. What matters most for the teacher is that he should keep his eyes open and his ears alert to what is really happening in the speech and writing of educated people. If he is willing to accept the remark of the Plowden Report, 'Speech is how people speak, not how some authority thinks they ought to speak',[2] he may find it possible to extend this tolerance to the children's writing.

More formal communication to children

We now have to look at the more formal uses of language, written and spoken, that are brought to a child, often at home, certainly in school. This more formal communication comes to him, not so much as from a single person to a single person but, rather, from a community of those who use or have used his mother tongue to him as a member of this community. It comes to him directly or through his teachers, in speech and in the written word.

First of all, books. All books? In one of his essays, Charles Lamb distinguishes between books and 'biblia a-biblia— books which are no books'; he banishes from the realm of true books, everything but imaginative literature: poems, plays, novels. Even history, which he specially mentions, is exiled.

Lamb's whimsical distinction is not altogether foreign to thinking and practice in some of our schools—most obviously at the secondary stage but by no means absent from junior schools. No teacher, it is true, would go so far with Lamb as to exclude travel, biography, history, geography from the realm of books; but they are often not felt to be 'literature'—as poetry and stories are. These are dealt with in a special way; for these, both form and content are felt to be important. But Lamb's 'non-books', plentiful though they may be in the class or school library, and however much they come into class-work, are usually read for their content, with little or no attention to their form.

In our study here we need take nothing for granted, and so we may ask what is implied by this difference of treatment. The implications, though rarely made explicit, can be stated as alternative views.

The more extreme implication is that only in imaginative literature is the form significant; that general style, language structures and vocabulary are essential elements only in the words of the poet, novelist or playwright. His communication with us is effective only if we respond to the intimate interaction between form and content. But in the books which are not imaginative literature, only the content matters; the form is irrelevant.

The alternative implication is not so extreme. It recognizes that in communication the form is always important, but takes it for granted that we need give no special attention to this in reading the books that are not imaginative literature. The training children receive in responding to form as well as content in 'literature' will carry over and be transferred to all their other reading. The implication is that it is in the study and 'appreciation of literature' that children learn to read in the fullest sense, and that the habits of approach and attention set up in this way will serve them whatever else they read.

But in addition to these two alternative approaches, there is a third possibility: to recognize that in everything that is read—not only imaginative literature—both form and content matter; that both are intrinsic elements in all formal communication.

Two things follow. First, let us say at once that this does not mean that in the junior school there must be deliberate attention to form in itself. In practice, it becomes a question of the art and skill of the teacher in evoking responses to form in relation to content.

Secondly, to do this the teacher must himself be aware of the different kinds of response that should be evoked by the different kinds of writing. In the junior school there will be only the beginnings of these; the teacher can be helped to see where he is going and where he is leading the children if he looks at fully-fledged mature communication in adult life. To get a clear perspective for aims and practices in the junior school he must look far ahead.

The range of formal communication

In recent years there has been a very important extension of literate communication: what was once the almost exclusive province of books has today become extended by a vast range of the spoken word. Every kind of writing now has its counterpart in spoken utterance, on radio or television, or recorded on disc or tape.

It is tempting to see this, as for instance McLuhan does, as a flight away from the written word, speech freed from the tyranny of the written alphabet.[3] But this is as yet an illusion. Most formal speech is literate, in the strict sense; it is bound to the written word. Maybe some truly unbound speech occurs in unscripted discussions and interviews or impromptu reports or statements. A great deal, however, that comes to us in public speech—from platform, radio or television—is no more than reading aloud; even though the writing is for the purpose of speaking. The cumulative effect is a vast extension of the formal spoken word. If we call Lamb's 'books' literature, we must say that today there is a growing spoken literature, as well as spoken formal communication corresponding to his non-books.

We have to go further still; we have to recognize that there is no hard-and-fast line between Lamb's books and his non-books. They have this in common, that all are forms of literate communication. If then we call the whole of this range of communication 'literature', we are not going beyond a normal modern usage, as the Oxford English Dictionary tells us. We can say that there is a spectrum of literature, written and spoken, extending from poetry to scientific communication.

For the teacher it becomes necessary to look closely at the different kinds of speech and writing within this spectrum of literature. He will see their likeness and differences most clearly if he looks at their fully-fledged forms in adult life. This is not, it need hardly be said, in order to bring his analysis into the classroom; but only in order that he himself may be clear about the directions in which he is hoping to lead his children.

The kinds of literate communication

Although there is no hard-and-fast line between imaginative literature and other books, we may suspect that there is a validity lurking beneath the distinction made by

Lamb and implied in the theory and practice of many teachers.

Everyone knows that fiction is not history. Nobody believes that there was once a man Lemuel Gulliver who went on a voyage to Laputa. Nobody who reads *War and Peace* expects an accurate account of Napoleon's Russian campaign. Children, long before they reach us in the junior school, are asking: Is it true? Did it really happen? Is it make-up? They are in no doubt that there is a difference between make-belief and belief.

This is the broad distinction as we pass from one end of the spectrum of literature to the other. Various terms are used to mark this distinction: imaginative and reproductive; creative and re-creative; emotive and referential; declarative and manipulative. Now if we look along the whole line of this spectrum—from poetry, plays and novels, through history and geography to scientific communication—what we find at any one point is not the entire absence of one in each of these pairs, but the dominance of one or the other.

The imaginative and the reproductive

Take, as a crucial example, the kind of work that, while still among Lamb's books, stands nearest to his dividing line: the historical novel. In *War and Peace*, Tolstoy tells his story of Pierre, Natasha and the rest, in and out of the Napoleonic War. How does this compare with a historical study of the War? Certainly we can say that the novel is more imaginative, creative, emotive and declarative than the history. But what is also clear is that both the novel and the history are all these as well as their opposites.

It would be absurd to say that the novel is purely imaginative, while there is nothing imaginative in the history. Of course Tolstoy brings in actual events, if only to anchor his story to time and place. Of course the historian has to draw upon his imagination, if only to interpret what has been said, written or done in the past. There is poetry in archaeology. The historical novel and the history are both imaginative and reproductive.

The creative and the re-creative

The basic difference between the novelist and the historian is a difference in total intention. The novelist aims at the creation of what might happen, the historian at the re-creation of what has happened. This difference of intention is reflected in every aspect of the work of communication. There are differences in the themes; differences in the processes by which the themes are developed; differences in the language used.

Yet there are likenesses. The novelist and the historian alike are not only both imaginative and reproductive, they are also both creative and re-creative.

The differences that are apparent between novels and history become of course more marked as we move to the extremes of the spectrum, when we see poetry in contrast with science. Yet there are likenesses here too. Obviously poetry is reproductive as well as imaginative, re-creative as well as creative. But what can we say of science?

There is no doubt that scientific thinking and communication often need to be imaginative and creative. A hypothesis is an imaginative leap forward—to be tested, it is true, by organized systematic observation, often in a situation experimentally devised for the purpose. The place of imagination throughout the process of scientific thinking has long been recognized by those scientists who are interested in their own methods of work and thought. Darwin, for instance, makes it clear in his *Autobiography* that in his hypothesis of evolution of species through natural selection he made an imaginative leap forward: from what he knew of the selective breeding of animals by man, to the idea of man himself being selectively bred by 'nature' through eons of time.[4] Today the processes of scientific thinking are receiving a great deal of attention; not least from men of science themselves. While they are no more in general agreement than poets about their work, we can certainly choose one who speaks for many. P. B. Medawar, the biologist, a Fellow of the Royal Society, says: 'A scientist must indeed be freely imaginative and yet sceptical; creative and yet a critic'.[5]

If we recognize the place of the imaginative and the creative, the reproductive and the re-creative, throughout the whole range of the spectrum of literature, we shall be less likely to over-emphasize one or the other in school. In some schools today there is a danger of giving 'creative' too narrow a meaning, an undue and disproportionate predominance and an artificial prestige, to the detriment of the re-creation and the presentation of what has actually happened and is happening. On the other hand, there is also an artificial prestige sometimes given to re-creative writing, because it is thought to be 'factual' and to abjure the flights of imagination. But a balanced education recognizes that the different modes within the spectrum of thought, feeling and presentation are complementary rather than the opposition or negation of each other.

The emotive and the referential

Nor, as is sometimes supposed, is there any simple opposition between the emotive and the referential (or 'symbolic') as Ogden and Richards used these terms. Since they first offered them, now nearly fifty years ago, there has been no little misinterpretation and misuse of them. They certainly distinguished between them as two functions of language: 'The symbolic use of words is statement; the recording, the support, the organization and the communication of references. The emotive use of words is a more simple matter; it is the use of words to express or excite feelings and attitudes'.[6] Subsequent discussion has replaced 'symbolic' by 'referential' and has tended to suggest that this and the emotive are mutually exclusive. But this was not the view of Ogden and Richards; they said quite explicitly that the two functions usually occur together.[7]

There is no doubt that this is so throughout the whole spectrum of literature, except perhaps where scientific statements are couched in their own special notation, verbal and mathematical. Here there is perhaps no emotive element; but as soon as we leave this extreme and move from the physical to the biological sciences, then on to sociological studies and so to history, we find a constant combination of the emotive with the referential.

This remains true even at the furthest extreme: all poetry is in some measure referential. In narrative poetry so much so, that in the classroom historical and geographical literalness may come to be the focus of attention.

> At Flores in the Azores Sir Richard Grenville lay
> And a pinnace, like a flutter'd bird, came flying from far away . . .

There is an obvious danger of over-emphasizing the referential in reading and responding to narrative poetry. Lyrical poetry, on the other hand, might seem to present the clearest instances, in all literature, of the wholly emotive. Wordsworth is often cited in support of this view. But when he said in the Preface to *Lyrical Ballads*: 'Poetry takes its origin from emotion recollected in tranquillity', can he have meant that even lyrical poetry is purely emotive? If so, this is belied by his own practice:

> I wandered lonely as a cloud
> That floats on high o'er vales and hills . . .

In these two lines every word is referential except perhaps 'lonely'.

It is true that Wordsworth was speaking of the origin of a poem, not of its final expression through the medium of words. His statement is, however, so liable to misinterpretation and so often quoted with deference to his authority, that T. S. Eliot thought it needed rebuttal. Wordsworth's statement, he says, is at best 'inexact'; and adds: 'The only way of expressing emotion in the form of art is by finding an "objective correlative"; in other words, a set of objects, a situation, a chain of events which shall be the *formula* of that particular emotion'.[8]

This recognition of the function of an objective correlative is certainly more 'exact' and complete than Wordsworth's statement. The cloud that floats on high o'er vales and hills is clearly an 'objective correlative' to the expression of the emotion of loneliness. If we translate this into the language of Ogden and Richards, we can say that the reference to the floating cloud becomes a means of expressing and evoking the emotion of loneliness: the referential aids the emotive.

The declarative and the manipulative

Finally we come to the two functions that we have seen emerging in earliest infancy and developing in everyday communication throughout childhood into adult life. The distinction between the declarative and the manipulative has something to add to the pairs of characteristics that we have just been speaking about.

The imaginative and reproductive, the creative and the re-creative—these emphasize the nature of the thinking and of the processes by which a theme is brought into communication. The emotive and referential: these draw attention to the language used and its relation to what is being communicated; its functions in expressing emotion and in referring to a situation.

The declarative and manipulative; these emphasize another aspect: the relations between the people engaged in communication—the speaker and the listener, the writer and the reader. The intentions and the effects of what is said may be declarative, the establishment of communion; or manipulative, the initiation of a task, mental or physical. And we notice that these relationships in communication occur at all points of the spectrum. Whether a work is mainly imaginative or reproductive, mainly creative or re-creative, mainly referential or emotive, it may also be mainly either declarative or manipulative in intention or in effect, or any combination of these.

A piece of scientific writing, referential in character and with a manipulative intention, may have something of a declarative effect on a reader. For many of us this is, for instance, what happens when we read Darwin's *Origin of Species*. While it is effective in its manipulative intention to set going a train of reasoning, for many of us there is also a declarative effect—we marvel, admire and are perhaps even moved by the magnitude of Darwin's conception. In this instance the declarative effect may reinforce the effect of the manipulative intention.

A poet, playwright or novelist, again, while engaging us in an imaginative experience, may realize that his work is likely to have a moral effect, and be aware of a conflict of intentions. While wishing his work to influence conduct—as Wordsworth, Shaw and Tolstoy all do—he sees the danger of weakening or distorting the imaginative experience for the sake of the message; the risk of impairing aesthetic integrity in the interest of the promotion of moral conduct.

Tolstoy, who often closely watched himself at work, testifies to this dilemma. In *What is Art?* he expresses what appears to have been a deeply-rooted conviction throughout his life as a writer: 'A perfect work of art will be one in which the content is important and significant to all men, and therefore it will be moral'.[9] But in another place he says:

> If I were told that I could write a novel in which I could indisputably establish as true my point of view on all social questions, I would not dedicate two hours to such a work. But if I were told that what I wrote would be read twenty years from now by those who are children today, and that they would weep and laugh over it and fall in love with the life in it, then I would dedicate all my existence and all my powers to it.[10]

The writer's dilemma is his recognition that he cannot ignore the possible ethical effects of his work; yet to have these effects it must succeed as an imaginative work. If *War and Peace* has done anything to affect our attitudes to war, it is because of the life that pulsates through its pages. If in *The Doll's House* or *An Enemy of the People* Ibsen himself says anything to us, it is because of their dramatic vigour and power. Some of Shaw's plays fail of their didactic intention because they are not good as plays. If for some people Wordsworth's poems fail of their moral intention, it is because they are not felt as poems.

A teacher in a junior school has a complementary problem in much of what he brings to his children. There is no possibility of eluding moral issues, since children of this age are deeply interested in right and wrong, particularly when these are embodied in the doings of actual people. The studies of Piaget and others bring us systematic observations of what can be seen every day in any home or classroom.[11] The children are, as yet, not well able to make—or indeed, are hardly interested in—general moral judgements based on impersonal ethical criteria. Direct moral preachments in a story pass over their heads; so that they can accept, without boredom or resentment, the unabashed didactic tales concocted for children in the past.

A teacher who is alert to what is happening to his children will often see that, because of the immaturity of their moral judgements, the discussion of the ethical implications of a story may distort these by reducing them to unduly simple and crude issues. But if he is willing to be guided by what he knows of problems of didacticism in adult literature, as well as of the ethical development of children, he is likely to be more successful if he lets the story make its own point.

Detailed questions of practice we again leave for Part III. In the meantime we have to look at one more aspect of the various kinds of literature—their forms in relation to their functions.

Forms and their functions

The word 'formal' has a wide range of meaning. To say that literature is more formal than everyday speech and writing, is to emphasize the part played by the form in the process of communication. It means that the writer or speaker has devoted thought and craftsmanship to form in his work: from the structure of the work as a whole—the pattern of the presentation of the themes—down to the individual words; and that there is a corresponding demand on the reader or listener to respond to the form. If it is a gross simplification and exaggeration to say, as McLuhan does, that the medium *is* the message,[12] it remains true that throughout the spectrum of literature the medium is an essential element in the message.

While it is always a means of presenting the theme, at the poetic end of the spectrum form has an additional function. Here form has its own aesthetic identity; it evokes an aesthetic response to itself as well as to the theme it serves to present. The pattern of a poem as a whole; stanza-form; rhythm; rhyme; the sounds of words; these singly and together have emotive power; they express the poet's enjoyment of his art in choosing or creating form.

One poet, at least, has stated for us his conviction of the supremacy of the form over the theme in poetry; A. E. Housman, in his famous lecture *The Name and Nature of Poetry*, writes: 'Meaning is of the intellect, poetry is not . . . Blake's meaning is often unimportant or virtually non-existent, so that we can listen with all our hearing to his celestial tune'.[13] It is the complete reversal of the Duchess's grave advice to Alice: 'Take care of the sense and the sounds will take care of themselves'.

Neither of these opposed views survives a balanced and temperate analysis in the philosophy of aesthetics. Samuel Alexander, for instance, gives full recognition to the emotive power both of the theme and the form in a poem. In *Beauty and Other Forms of Value* he distinguishes between the emotions evoked by the theme and the emotive effect of the form. This he calls 'artistic emotion' or 'aesthetic passion'. 'The whole pleases in successful art, because it satisfies the aesthetic passion'. This passion may be evoked by every detail of form, down to the forms of words, which 'become the material of art when they are used not for the sake of the things which they mean but in themselves and for their own sake'. Where there is emotive force in the form as well as emotive force in the theme, each enhances the other and at the same time each exercises its own particular power. Thus the aesthetic emotion and the emotions evoked by the theme 'are, in great art, felt in their unity and discrimination; hopeless sorrow in Lear's lines on the Fool's death'.[14]

When, by contrast, we turn to the scientific end of the spectrum, we see the forms solely as an instrument in the presentation of the theme. Here they can be said to exist not at all for their own sake but to serve to communicate an orderly progress of thought in such a way as to promote a similar progress in the mind of the reader or listener.

As an aid to this ordered presentation, scientific communication frequently finds it essential to supplement the resources of language by non-linguistic means of exhibiting the patterns of thought. So used, charts, maps and other diagrams are not merely casual adjuncts to language, more or less dispensable; they become intrinsically valuable means of presenting ideas, effective throughout that part of the spectrum which ranges from the physical sciences right up to and including human history.

Light is thrown on the distinctive functions of diagrams if we compare them, as illustrations, with pictures. While pictures add to and enhance the concreteness of themes, emphasizing their impact on the senses, diagrams abstract from this concreteness, by depicting the relationships and the sequences of thoughts. Each in its own way reinforces the effects of the words. The television screen is so potent a means of communication, not, as is sometimes said, because it is visual, non-verbal. Its power is in the force of the combination of the graphic with the verbal; of pictures and diagrams with words. For the teacher it offers an opportunity to study the different and complementary functions of these diverse instruments of communication: words spoken and written, pictures, diagrams.

Differences of vocabulary

Finally we look at differences of vocabulary within the spectrum of literature: semantic differences and differences in the repertory of words.

Semantic differences we have earlier glanced at, in our instance of *ten thousand*, as used in everyday conversation and by Wordsworth. We now need to take this kind of comparison further and observe more closely the differences in the meanings of the 'same' word, as used in everyday communication, in scientific and in poetic literature. We put the word 'same' in inverted commas to indicate the fact that when a word—a particular phonetic or alphabetic pattern—has a variety of meanings, these are functionally different words.

The possibility of ignoring these differences is greatest with the words that are most familiar. Take, for instance, the word 'mother', used and encountered by us in so many contexts and registers. In infancy, as we have seen, the meaning of the word lies in its direction towards a particular person. Before the end of his first year a child may be using 'mama' with the effect of communicating with his mother, declaratively or manipulatively or both. At this stage the word—the sound-pattern—would seem to be no more than a vocal gesture, a vocal act by which he draws attention to his needs. What these needs are, his mother recognizes from his intonation, facial expression, bodily behaviour, the circumstances and much else. While then 'mama' draws her attention to one need or another, it is unlikely that as early as this the word is, for the child, a name for anything. In Ogden and Richards' terms, the word is as yet hardly referential in the child's usage.

That a change is taking place becomes evident when—as in the case mentioned in Chapter 2—on seeing a picture of a woman a child gleefully says 'Mama!'[15] This has now something of a referential use—the word is on the way to becoming a name. For some time it will then have this function of naming a person; the next stage will be the extension of the meaning of the word to refer to a relationship between persons—between the child himself and his mother, between her and his sisters and brothers. If we ask what kind of relationship this is likely to be for the child, the answer beyond doubt is that at first it is emotional; love, care, protection from his mother; confidence, security, sometimes aggression, from him—

mainly orectic relationships. It may be long before the
range of word's meaning includes any notion of the
biological relationship of mother and child.

In the spectrum of literature, the meaning of the word
varies within this wide semantic range from the more
orectic to the more cognitive. It may be as orectic as in

> Land of hope and glory
> Mother of the free.

Or, at the other extreme, it may be as biological as the
Oxford Dictionary definition: 'a woman who has given
birth to a child'. These are the extremes; nearer the middle
of the spectrum—in a novel, for instance, or historical
writing—the semantic scope is likely to include both the
orectic and the biological relationship.

Meaning, description and definition

Now a very important part of a child's linguistic development is that he moves towards the ranges of meaning which
words—or phrases or sentences—have in adult life. This
process, which of course is always going on throughout a
child's schooling, becomes clearer if we look back at its
beginnings in infancy.

The examples we have just had of the meanings of
'mother' remind us that in the development of the meaning
of a word, one of the most powerful factors is the *context
of language* in which we encounter it. In the beginnings, in
early infancy, the context of a heard word can only be
non-verbal; that is, the actual situation in which it occurs.
But very little time passes before a context of words invades
the non-verbal situation. A child, for instance, first learns
to respond to 'Mummy' in virtue of the circumstances in
which he hears and he himself utters it: the sight, sound—
even the smell—of his mother; when he is uncomfortable,
hungry or sleepy; when she brings him his milk; when she
plays with him.

Soon, in her ordinary natural talk to him, she says things
like 'Mummy's coming!' 'Mummy's bringing baby's milk!'

'Mummy tuck him in!' 'Mummy give him his ball'. It is this kind of verbal context which, at first affording only the slightest clue to meaning, gradually increases its contribution. There comes a time when a word is encountered in a purely verbal context; in stories, for instance: 'There was a girl who lived in a castle . . . What's a castle, Mother?' There are even words for which there can be only verbal contexts: *if, but, although, however* and the rest.

Coming back to *mother*, we see that in different parts of the spectrum of literature verbal contexts have different functions. Broadly speaking, at the poetic end contexts illustrate; at the scientific end, contexts define. For instance, the poetic meaning of *mother* develops for a child through a series of verbal contexts which illustrate its orectic meaning—a series of contexts which depict emotional personal relationships. On the other hand, the scientific meaning of this word develops through a series of contexts which define its biological, non-orectic, relationships; *female, birth, child* are words which obtain their meaning by being put into relationships with a network of concepts; and this is what definition is.

The difference between illustration and definition is important. *Mother of the free*—it is impossible to embrace the orectic content of this by definition; just as it is impossible to embrace the biological content of *birth* and *child* by illustration. These are different techniques of explanation through contexts of words. To be aware of these techniques does not of course mean that they are to be crudely deployed in the classroom. They should come to the children not as procedures to be singled out for special attention; they should, rather, be guides to the teacher himself in ensuring that the range of the children's linguistic experience—in listening and reading—is wide enough to include both the contexts which illustrate and the contexts which define.

For, in the end, the meanings of words develop for a child as he encounters them in a diversity of contexts, non-verbal as well as verbal; and as he endeavours to use them himself. It is this side of his linguistic experience that we now go on to consider.

Notes

[1] Gowers (1962), pp. 198, 206.
[2] Central Advisory Council for Education (England) (1967), p. 222.
[3] McLuhan (1964).
[4] Darwin (1929), p. 57.
[5] Medawar (1967), p. 118.
[6] Ogden and Richards (1949), p. 149.
[7] Ogden and Richards (1949), p. 150.
[8] Eliot (1928), pp. 58, 100.
[9] Tolstoy (1929), p. 56.
[10] Tolstoy (1957), Introduction.
[11] Lewis (1963), p. 138 and references there to Piaget, Peel and Johnson.
[12] McLuhan (1964).
[13] Housman (1933), pp. 38, 40.
[14] Alexander (1933), pp. 130, 38.
[15] The changes are summarized in Lewis (1963), p. 37.

Chapter Four

The Child Using Language

LINGUISTIC experience is not only what is brought to a child in communication. We now have to look at the speech and writing that comes from the child: first, in communication, secondly, in his private language.

Communication from the child

The children are speaking or writing; what are they doing, what are we doing? We have to take a fresh look at what has become almost too familiar to notice. We see that a child may be doing one of two very different things: re-producing what has previously been brought to him or producing something of himself, spontaneously.

Traditionally, the school has been mainly concerned with the first kind of speech or writing—a child's re-production of what he has previously heard or read. The possibility that a child might have something to offer from his own resources became a practical question only when teachers began to urge the introduction of the mother tongue into the classical curriculum; in this country in the sixteenth century. But even those who insisted most strongly on the importance of the mother tongue in education thought it absurd to expect anything in the way of spontaneous writing from a child. In 1612, we find John Brinsley, a vigorous pioneer for the admission of English into the grammar school, saying this: 'For telling a child that he must invent variety of matter of his owne head, to write to his friend; this is a taske overhard for ordinary wits. For what can a child have in his understanding, to be able to conceive or write of, which he hath not read or in some way knowne before?' [1]

The principle here may seem only acceptable when schooling is equivalent to teaching Latin; but there is something to be said for it, however wide the curriculum. It must always be important for a teacher to be able to estimate what his pupils have grasped; and to get them to try to reproduce it is an obvious way of doing so. But it is only too easy to be convinced that what is convenient for us must be good for our children. The principle of linking children's own use of language with what they read has persisted, though in a less trenchant form than Brinsley's. A recognition of the value of books readily overflows into a belief that literature and writing are inseparable in school. We see this happening in a symposium published in 1946 under the very respectable aegis of The English Association.

> But though boys and girls are voluble enough in certain directions, their interests are naturally narrow, so that the range of topics for composition to be drawn from their own experience is limited . . . It is therefore most desirable that work in composition—especially in the earlier stages—should be linked with the study of literature . . . From this point of view it is a mistake to discuss the teaching of composition in separation from the teaching of literature: the two go hand in hand.[2]

Three-hundred and fifty years since Brinsley; twenty years since the English Association statement; surely there must be something in a tradition as persistent as this. But we, here, have to ask: How does this tradition fit in with the principle so strongly supported by research and investigation, as we have outlined these in Part I: that the mother tongue has a special place in a child's development, influenced by and influencing his thought, feeling and action?

This principle clearly leads directly to an emphasis on spontaneous speech and writing—'self-expression', creation. Our question then becomes: In what circumstances, what conditions, can each of these functions of language, the re-productive and the productive, contribute to a child's thought, feeling and action—more exactly, to his cognitive and orectic development?

Now whenever we test the soundness of any practice in education, there are always two criteria; first, its value in a child's life, satisfying his needs here and now; secondly, its value in preparation for his adult life. About each of the two functions of language we have to ask: What can it do for a child within the school; what for him out of school; what in preparation for his life as an adult?

The values of reproductive communication

There is one obvious difference when a child is speaking in school and out of it: his relation to his audience. Out of school, when a child is speaking with people, he and they have the same kind of intention—to arouse and influence thought, feeling and action. But in school, while this is still the teacher's intention, the children are often called upon to do something essentially different—to reproduce.

To many teachers—to more and more probably in recent years—this is highly repugnant; they see reproduction as dull, old-fashioned, authoritarian; useful maybe to the teacher but stultifying to children in their urge to express themselves, to create, to produce. It is the kind of question on which teachers take sides—the new versus the old, the progressive versus the conservative, freedom versus compulsion, and so on. Our business here, again taking nothing for granted, is to see what there is to be said for this time-honoured practice of reproduction as a means of developing a child's language and as an influence on his development as a thinking person.

We can certainly say that the practice of reproductive speech and writing stands up well to the test of the two criteria of educational value.

On its immediate value for a child here and now it can be fully justified. Not only is it indispensable in the classroom. Out of school it may also play an important part in children's development, linguistic and general. Every day at home we ask our children whether they understand or remember; what we are doing is inviting them to put into words what has come to them in words; what they have heard, later also what they have read. The kind of language the child uses is influenced by the language he has encountered, not only in its forms but also in what it communicates, and the level of abstractness and concreteness in its thought, very much as Bernstein has pointed out.

But this is not simply imitation. What began in infancy, as the combination of imitation with exploration, continues throughout childhood. In attempting to reproduce what has come to him in words, a child usually has to do more than merely repeat these words. Adapting himself to his listener he often has to reconstruct his past experience. This is a skill worth cultivating, not only because it is useful in childhood but also because in adult life we are constantly being called upon to give an account of what we have heard or read; and this remains one of the main uses of language.

With so much to be said for reproductive communication, it is not surprising that it continues to play such a large part in the classroom.

The values of productive communication

Yet it would be shortsighted to allow reproductive communication to be the main aim in school. For it falls short, in a very important way, of the kind of communication which becomes more and more necessary to a child as he grows up and is of supreme importance to him in his adult life: productive communication, aimed at evoking thought or feeling or both in another person. In reproductive communication in school the incentive, whether admitted or not, is to satisfy the teacher, to discover what he wants you to say and to say it. In productive communication the incentive for the speaker is to satisfy himself—that he is successful in communicating something new to his listener. He is trying to tell someone what he has been doing, or what he would like his listener to do, or is 'sharing his feelings' with his listener. If this kind of relationship is absent, or rare, in the classroom, one result—often only too obvious—is the apathy, the listless lack of energy and interest, if ever the children are called upon to communicate their own experiences. It is as if they are still asking themselves: 'What does he want me to say?' instead of, 'What do I want to say?'

In their everyday life, out of school, children are constantly called upon, encouraged, to speak in this productive way. We say casually: 'Well, was it a nice party?' or, 'How did you like your visit to the fire-station?' or, after a game, 'How did it go?' or, after a TV session, 'What have you been looking at?' The child's answers lead to more questions from us and so quite naturally a whole sequence of his experiences is put into words.

That this is important practice in the use of language is beyond question. The child is put into the position of having to communicate so as to make himself understood, and at every moment his success is put to the test by the come-back from his listener. And while he is practising the skills of speaking, some of his words have already been part of the experiences described—what people said at the party; what the firemen said; what the people said in the TV play.

Through this a child may increase his ability to verbalize his past experiences, both overt and inner. In verbalizing past overt experiences, the words not only help him to recall what has happened but also to organize and put the events in order for future use. Recalling the past helps him to anticipate and plan the future.

Again, if we may follow Piaget and Vigotsky, the use of words in recalling overt experiences may, as it becomes inner language, serve the needs of thoughts and feelings. Inner language may thus help a child to organize these and, as Luria and his associates have insisted, help to regulate them.[3]

The practical implications are clear. While we must not underestimate the importance of reproductive communication, it is even more important to provide for a full development of productive communication. In the classroom the problem is to secure a real audience for a child speaking or writing. It is incomparably easier to get a child to give back what he has had from the teacher than for him to feel he has an audience to talk or write to about his own concerns. What this amounts to in practice we look at in Part III.

Private language

Not all the language we normally use is communication with another person. As we go about our daily concerns we 'think aloud'; more often we speak silently to ourselves—and this is still overt language. Most of all, literate as we now have become, a good deal of an ordinary person's everyday writing is private, for his own benefit. He makes notes of what has happened; perhaps he keeps an address book; he makes memoranda to enable him to plan ahead. He is communicating with his future self; he writes with himself in view as the future reader of what he is now writing. This is private language which, while recording the past, has a forward intention.

There is also private language which has no reference at all to the past but is directed only to the future. A shopping list, an engagement book, are simple examples. More elaborate instances are notes of a proposed course of action: the itinerary of a holiday, the outline of a speech to be made or of an important letter to be written.

But not all private language is communication with oneself. Sometimes it is of the kind that accompanies present action and is intimately interwoven with it, very much like the 'synpractic' language of infancy and childhood. We say to ourselves such things as: 'Now, where did I put that hammer?' like the small boy looking for his piece of string. There may be this difference: that as in adult life there is something of a social taboo on talking aloud to oneself, we do it silently. But its functions are essentially no different from those of the synpractic language of childhood. This private language may act as an aid to a course of action. It may help to direct and order a course of thinking. Sometimes to put pen to paper is to stimulate thought; sometimes by trying to say what we think, we find out what we are thinking. Private language may also have orectic effects, helping to clarify and order our feelings, wishes and intentions.

Few people make no use at all of these aids; for many of us they are indispensable. Now since they have these uses both in adult life and in infancy, it would be strange if this were not true of the intervening period, childhood. The question of what place private language may have in the primary school we can put to the test of our two criteria of educational value: immediate, for the benefit of the children here and now; future, in preparation for adult life.

Now, in a number of traditional customary practices in primary schools we do find attempts to use something like private language as an aid to various processes of education. Once the children have some command of the written word, there are routine classroom uses of what may be called semi-private language.

The earliest use of synpractic written language in the junior school is in arithmetic, as soon as the children begin to set down their sums on paper. The lines of figures, which are a notation for doing the arithmetic, often become an aim in themselves and are even felt to *be* arithmetic. Most teachers are, however, familiar with the change of attitude which is taking place in the beginnings of mathematics, the realization that figures and words are essentially a means for *thinking* arithmetic.

This throws some light on the place of written private language in its wider uses in the junior school. Private language comes in as soon as children begin to jot down words that help them in their thinking. Obvious uses are planning a class expedition or plotting the dramatization of a story to be acted in class. But, here again, when the teacher takes a hand, and what the child writes is semi-private rather than private, it may become an end in itself, instead of an aid to thinking and planning.

No doubt it is natural for a teacher to want to keep an eye on what each child is doing—at the least, to see that he is doing something to the point, at best to help him to avoid mistakes and use his words to the best advantage. No doubt it is also natural for a teacher to want the children's work to be neat and tidy and generally presentable. Yet these aims, innocuous and even desirable for many of the other things done in school, can be just disastrous to any real use of private language. This should be an instrument, a means to an end—helping individual thought, feeling and action. If the *form* of private language is made an end in itself, it may lose its chief instrumental value.

What happens then is that imitation has taken the place of initiative. The writing has demanded of the children no more energy than is needed to follow and satisfy their teacher; it has given them little or no practice in using private language—whether as an aid to recall for future reference, or as a map or blueprint of future action, or as a mode of action in the present. Thus, while there is the outward form of private language, a child's experience may well be deprived of one of its main values; whether for his education within the school, for his everyday life out of school or by way of preparation for his adult life.

We have here one more instance of a dilemma which recurs in school education: to help a child to acquire skills which, while they are intended for the conditions of life beyond the school, are shaped by the conditions of life within the school. The characteristics of adult private language are out of keeping with what is normally acceptable in school. Since it is not primarily intended for communication with others, it does not aim at being presentable in public. It may have no obvious shape or pattern. With false starts, short cuts and unrectified mistakes, it may be illegible, in a private shorthand or code of symbols, and unintelligible to anyone but the writer himself.

These are characteristics in direct opposition to all that a school usually and rightly aims at in the cultivation of writing for communication: that it should be legible, intelligible, as free as possible of ambiguities due to errors, and with a due attention to form. It is not surprising, therefore, if some teachers—though with a full intention of helping children to use a private language—are insensibly led to assimilate their methods and criteria to those suitable for communicative language. They expect the same attention to spelling, punctuation and general neatness in the children's private language.

On the other hand, the classroom inevitably demands some modification of private language. School, however closely concerned with children's everyday needs and their future as adults, cannot be a simple copy of life beyond its walls, still less of adult life. The school aims at developing in children skills that will enable them to perform tasks in the outside world, but it must do this in conditions different from those of the outside world. The children are confined in a specially devised and equipped environment, they are in company with other children, under adults with whom they have the peculiar relationship of pupil to teacher. These are conditions within which linguistic education, like all other education, must go on.

Here we are concerned with a particularly delicate task for the school: to promote children's use of private language. Yet it can rarely be private from the teacher, and for the most part should not be. Whilst, then, it is public to him, he has to be careful not to impair its special functions as private language. The consequent practical problems for the teacher we take up in Part III.

Notes

[1] Brinsley (1612), p. 167.
[2] Pink (1946), p. 88.
[3] Luria (1961), p. 59; descriptions of experiments with infants are in Luria (1959).

PART III

In the Classroom

Chapter Five

Some Fundamental Principles of Practice

IN THIS chapter we attempt to put forward some basic principles which seem to be valid in the cultivation of the mother tongue in the junior school and which are implied in the practice of many experienced teachers. Here we ask what light is thrown on these principles by research and thought about children and about language; we attempt to relate them to what we know about the development of language and what we can see of its functions in adult life.

Divergence between teacher and child

Before we look at these principles we must remind ourselves of a fundamental fact of the relationship of a teacher with his pupils. While their co-operation is essential for the success of everything the school undertakes, there is a basic divergence in interests, intentions and goals. The teacher looks forward to his pupils' future; they are mainly concerned with the here-and-now. A child may have dreams about his future, but they are likely to be only dreams, without the potency to determine what he does today. It is the teacher who brings the possible future to bear upon the actual present.

The reconciliation of these divergences is a test of the skill and wisdom of a teacher. He has somehow to combine

his concern for the children's interests and their life today
with attention to their future needs. This is not easy. It is
much easier to over-emphasize the importance of one of
the two factors at the expense of the other: to say, 'Look
after the child's present interests and the future will look
after itself'; or to say, 'We must be ready to sacrifice a
child's present interests for the sake of his future welfare'.
At its crudest, the antithesis is expressed in well-known
opposed extremes; the child-centred as against the subject-
centred school.

This is still a live issue; as the Plowden Committee found,
still worth discussing.[1] Research into the history of educational thought and practice has something to contribute
here. To understand the position today it is illuminating to
look back and ask when and why each of these two opposed
views was valid; and whether any change in human affairs
makes either view less valid now.

The subject-centred curriculum has a long tradition. It
has sometimes been misrepresented as neglecting the
welfare of the children; on the contrary, it was because
teachers and parents were concerned about the future that
the children were kept to a prescribed, well-tried, curriculum.
Etymologically a 'curriculum' is a race-course; the teacher,
by one means or another, trained his pupils to stand up to
the pace and the heavy going. For the successful the future
was assured; there were worthy prizes to be won. What
these could be was explained—in all sincerity, we are told—
in the famous claim for classical education in an early
nineteenth-century sermon at Oxford:

> The advantages of a classical education are twofold: it
> enables us to look down on those who have not shared its
> advantages, and also fits us for places of emolument not only
> in this world, but also in that which is to come.

This is an easy target for satire, but as an aim of education
it is not to be lightly dismissed. In fact, what is here
claimed for a classical education remains—with due changes
—the value of education in the minds of many people today.
No doubt the assertion is not presented in such stark nudity,

but decently veiled in a modern idiom it still commands
the assent of many parents, for whom the object of school
is not only to give Tom a better chance in life, but a better
chance than the boy next door. Education for prestige.
There is no doubt that one objection to the comprehensive
school is that it appears to remove the possibility of feeling
superior to those who have had an inferior brand of
education. Prestige in education comes to depend on
qualifications which open the door to better chances in life.
'O' levels and 'A' levels come to be valued because they
are the Open Sesame to success; the right curriculum is
the curriculum that provides the pupil with this.

For us here the importance of this view of education is
that whatever is done at the secondary stage must pro-
foundly influence policy and practice in the junior school.
In modern terms, the subject-centred curriculum offers its
own pragmatic justification, its practical effects in the
child's future, in answer to the parent's question: 'What will
be the outcome of this education for my child when he
grows up?'.

The Open Sesame view of education has therefore much
to commend it; it obviously falls short when it is not
enough concerned with a child's immediate needs. It is
this concern which leads to the child-centred school, which
also has a respectable tradition. It goes back at least as far
as Pestalozzi and has always made a special appeal to those
who like to feel themselves progressive and liberal-minded.
The Plowden Report regards it as a 'general and quickening
trend' today to recognize 'that the best preparation for
being a happy and useful man or woman is to live fully as
a child'.[2]

Many thoughtful parents, while attracted by the 'progressive' trend, are suspicious of it. They feel, no doubt,
that it is a dangerous concession to their inclination to
indulge their children; they fear to be experimental where
the welfare of the children may be at stake; that 'living
fully as a child' is a vague prescription compared with the
solid certainty of a well-tried curriculum.

For the teacher there is a real dilemma here: to reconcile his concern for the children's present needs with his concern for their future. It is a dilemma not to be resolved by blurring the differences and talking vaguely about maintaining a balance. The dilemma is real and has real practical issues in the cultivation of the mother tongue, where by the nature of things we are compelled to give attention to both present and future.

On the one hand, we cannot avoid the hard facts that the children, at whatever level of competence, have strongly-established habits in their mother tongue, and that they have present needs to satisfy through the medium of this language. On the other hand there is also the hard fact that the children's linguistic future is to some extent with them here and now. They live in an adult world; among, though not yet members of, an adult community which both attracts them to conformity with it and incites them to rebel against it.

What hope is there for a teacher to resolve the dilemma of present needs and future values? We would suggest that first he must see that there is a dilemma. He must recognize that his purposes are not the same, and cannot be the same, as the incentives for the children and their intentions. It becomes self-deception, dangerous to the children's education, for him to pretend that he is a child with them, with their immediate interests; nor can he expect them to share his concern for their future as adults. It is his business to keep an eye on their future, and from this duty he cannot abdicate. Yet he has to meet the children on their own ground, and from this must help them to move forward.

Compared with his predecessor at the beginning of the century, the teacher of today should have a sharper awareness of his dual role in attempting to satisfy the child's immediate needs as well as his future needs. To help him, the teacher will have some results of investigations into the place of language in the child's development, and some results of research into the structures and functions of language in its adult use. It is here that he is at an advantage compared with what he may be trying to do at other moments in the children's school life. When he is with them in junior school history or geography, or the beginnings of mathematics or a science, he can have little idea of what parts these may play in their developed forms, in the children's lives as adults. But in a child's linguistic education, the future is present now in the adult language, with its structures and its functions, in communication and in private. They are familiar to the teacher, and open to his everyday observation and study; and he can, if he wishes, get a fuller knowledge of them from the professional students of language—not only the linguists but the psychologists, the psycholinguists, the sociologists and the philosophers. He will know that the forms of a language are not changeless, static; and that in any society it is the young who are the chief agents of linguistic change.[3]

The teacher may think of his job as teaching English, very much as he might be teaching, say, the beginnings of history or geography. In fact, his task is essentially different; it is to continue and promote the children's linguistic development, which began long before they came to school. In order to do this he must learn from them as well as from the studies of children in general. How this knowledge is to be reflected in practice may be expressed in a number of basic principles which we now have to consider.

1. Linguistic education is continued development

The basic difference between the cultivation of the mother tongue and much else that goes on in school is implied in the remark in the Norwood Report that English is more than a subject. If this is to be accepted, it is not because it reflects a romantic glamour and a factitious prestige that some teachers of English like to feel about their special job. To say that the mother tongue is more than a school subject is to recognize a solid, down-to-earth principle, based on fact; to be neglected at the risk of debilitating what should be a vital and vigorous growth.

The fact that differentiates the cultivation of the mother tongue from nearly everything else that happens in school is this: that by the time a child comes to us his language is already well developed. Even if he is retarded he will have some language habits and skills already established. As for children in general, everyday observation suggests that by the age of eight they have a considerable command of the forms and usages of the mother tongue; and this is supported by special investigations such as that by Templin, mentioned in Chapter 1. As might be expected, it is in the development of meaning that eight-year-olds still have far to go, both in the vocabulary they use and in the vocabulary they respond to.[4]

In the mastery, therefore, of forms in the children's language the school can do no more than modify a highly developed hierarchy of skills and draw upon a complexity of deeply-rooted habits, interests and purposes. The task of the school is to enlarge the range of the functions of language and increase the ability of the children to discriminate among them, in using and in responding to language.

Every child has a powerful need to be understood and to understand others; we can take this as an axiom. He has some means, however imperfect, of communication; we can take this as a fact. What comes to him in his linguistic education is an elaboration of these means. The extension of his vocabulary, the development of meaning, the command of structures, the response to forms—all these develop from what is already there. In the extension of his vocabulary, many new meanings are received in the context of those that he already has; the new words are assimilated·to or discriminated from those which are already in his repertory. To go back to one of our earlier examples, he may have the word *table* by the time he is three; now in the junior school he comes on an extension of its meaning in 'Knights of the Round Table' and has to distinguish a new meaning in 'time-table' and '(multiplication) table'. Something of the same kind of combination of the new with the old occurs in the command of grammatical structures. A child of eight does not acquire completely new kinds of structures—he learns to use those he already possesses in a more discriminative way. He learns, for instance, to use *fast* in the two ways that later on he will name adjective and adverb. And if, in poetry for instance, he enjoys sounds and verbal patterns, this again goes on as a continued development of that enjoyment of the sounds and patterns of speech, the rudimentary beginnings of which we see in babbling in early infancy.[5] Thus we can say that a child's linguistic development in school is as much a diversification of his linguistic knowledge and skill as his introduction to anything new.

All this will be familiar to an experienced and perceptive teacher. Here, in support of this everyday observation, we have brought such evidence as we have of children's early development to suggest that the main processes continue into childhood in the junior school.

A practical corollary is that when a teacher sets to work from the existing habits and skills of a child, he may have to overcome active resistance to change. There is clear evidence that this is a recurring problem in linguistic education.[6] A child's mother tongue is the language that from birth he grows up with and into; and so deeply-rooted is this in each of us that we are highly sensitive to any suggestion that it is inferior or inadequate and needs to be modified or changed.

Yet precisely against this depth of feeling and habit it is a main purpose of the school to effect change in the children's mother tongue. It is clear, then, that rather than teaching them a 'subject'—English—our aim must be described as guiding the progressive continuation of their linguistic development.

2. Matter rather than form the ostensible aim for the child

The principle that linguistic education is continued development implies a second divergence between teacher and children. Putting this as a sharp antithesis—perhaps over-sharp—we say that he is interested in form, they in matter. There is the plain fact that when a child speaks he intends to say *something*; that when he listens he wants to understand *what* is being said; that when he uses private language it is as an aid to what he is doing, thinking, feeling. His interest in forms is secondary to his concern with meaning.

As we have seen, the child's powerful and unremitting concern with language arises out of his need to communicate; it is under this incentive that he rapidly achieves a command of the structures of the mother tongue. As a subsidiary incentive for attention to the forms of language he may be influenced by the standards set by his elders or his contemporaries. He may accept or reject what is said to be polite or vulgar or slang or modern or 'square'. But the main incentive for the development of his language will remain his need to say something to somebody.

By contrast, his teacher, from the nature of his task in cultivating the children's linguistic development, tends to be concerned with form rather more than with matter. Much of what they say or write, much of what he says to them or brings to them from others—much if not all of this is already familiar to him. Of course, up to a point he is interested in what they have to say, but as a teacher of English he is much more interested in how they say it. When they speak or write he will be concerned to improve their command of the language; when, under his guidance, they listen or read, he will wish to sharpen their responsive awareness of the language and enhance their sensibility to its forms.

The traditional concern in school with the forms of language has in recent years provoked a marked swing towards a greater concern with content. The Plowden Report, for instance, says that teachers should be at least as much concerned with the content as with the manner of what is said.[7] '*Should*'; our question here is: 'Why should they?'. Research gives no direct answer; but it can throw some light on how undue attention to form or to content may affect children's linguistic education.

(*i*) *Undue attention to form* is likely to slow down, if not impair, linguistic development because it bears a relatively weak incentive for children. If attention to form predominates over concern with meaning, and becomes analytical and abstract, it is boring to most children. Time is spent in the classroom at a low level of concern; time that might be given to the energetic use and enjoyment of language.

The most obvious example is grammar, which retains its place in schools not only because of its age-long tradition in education but because to many people it still appears to offer practical—even indispensable—advantages. A glance at its historical importance lights up its position today. As the name grammar school reminds us, the study of grammar was for centuries the natural centre of the curriculum. The key to a valued culture, classical literature, a key in the possession of the few, it bore a prestige, a mystique and a glamour. Etymologically 'glamour' is a form of 'grammar'.

What is the place of grammar today in the linguistic education of children? We have the odd position that the teaching of grammar flourishes in many schools, in the face of the most cogent arguments that it is useless and so a waste of valuable time. The issue is still so much alive as to bear the repetition of what has been said again and again during the last fifty years. It would be far from the truth to say that the formal study of grammar has been banished from the junior school. It is still necessary for the Plowden Report to maintain that it 'will have little place in the primary school, since active and imaginative experience and use of the language should precede attempts to analyse grammatically how language behaves'.[8] Again we ask: 'Why *should?*'.

For us here it is not enough to accept or reject the study of grammar in the junior school; we have to ask what light has research to throw upon the question. We have to look at practices in the light of what we know—little though it may be—of children and of language.

A possible justification for grammar in the education of children in their mother tongue may lie in the psychology of learning a skill. It seems reasonable to say that to acquire a skill a learner must be aware of the techniques—that is, have them put into words. This would certainly seem true of many skills in school, from arithmetic to woodwork—though recent attempts to improve the beginnings of mathematics have made us realize how delicate the balance must be between carrying out operations and putting them into words.[9] For some skills the relationship seems simpler. At school, learning to saw in the workshop, we were taught 'Hold tight, saw light!'—and this still often comes back to me to guide my hand. Since the mother tongue is a body of skills, can we not help the children by stating the principles underlying the formation of its structures; that is, its grammar?

The answer is that the mother tongue is different from other skills in the way in which it is acquired. From our observation of children, systematic as well as casual, it is pretty clear how they find their way into the structures of the living current language. As we have briefly indicated, they adapt their own schematic patterns of utterance to those of the current language by processes of which they are largely unaware. They learn to speak and respond to grammatical English without the study of English grammar. The syntax and accidence of the mother tongue, as they encounter these in their experience, become theirs in the course of this experience. As one modern linguist, speaking for many, puts it: 'the rules are known implicitly, even though they cannot be stated explicitly'.[10] By the time the children reach us in school they have such a mastery of the highly complex structural systems of language that the study of grammar can add little or nothing to their skill. Grammar becomes another of the things done in school; and their teachers find it no easier than they do to relate grammar to the use and comprehension of the mother tongue.

The question of grammar in the junior school is obscured by two things. First, when a child comes to a second language—and no methods however 'direct' can make its acquisition identical with the development of the mother tongue—he cannot go very far without some knowledge of the grammar of the new language. Teachers find that comparison with the grammar of the mother tongue is often helpful, sometimes indispensable.

Secondly, we must bear in mind that some schools maintain they are teaching grammar when in fact what they do is to draw the children's attention to grammatical English. This attention is something that many children enjoy and all need. Many are certainly interested in the regularities and pecularities of language and enjoy mastering them. But this is not the same thing as the study of the syntax and accidence of English, still less is it the traditional classroom games of 'analysis' and 'parsing' that children learn to play.

The interest that many children have in grammatical regularities is another aspect of that enjoyment of the forms of language which begins as the babbling of infancy. This can develop into a pleasure in the phonetic, intonational, rhythmical and structural patterns of language so important in imaginative literature; but we have to take care that giving children knowledge about forms does not take the place of aesthetic enjoyment of them. This is a delicate growth that may quickly wither if prematurely forced.

Certainly one of the chief dangers of an undue attention to form may be seen in its possibly inhibitory effect on children's own speech or writing.

I remember seeing a vigorous young teacher with a class of bright nine-year-olds. It was a morning in spring and she was trying to get them to talk about a bowl of daffodils on her table. They were interested and co-operative.

'Now, Mary', she said to a girl at the back of the class, 'What are you going to tell us?'

Mary stood up a little shyly and said something about the daffodils. 'That's very nice, Mary; but aren't there too many *ands* in your sentence?'

This sounds innocuous enough and something any one of us is capable of saying. But how deadly and how deadening; especially to a child already self-conscious and only too anxious to do what teacher seems to want.

(*ii*) *Undue attention to content.* With a realization of the difficulty and the dangers of an undue emphasis on form, a teacher may easily be led to an undue concern with content. The consequent gain in incentive for the children and in their liveliness and activity may be so great that he may well be forgiven for believing that all is well.

But this may be at the cost of something no less important, the children's need to grow to realize the relationship between content and form. This is a realization not to be gained by talking about it, but in the practice of language.

Samuel Butler, who never lost an opportunity of a thrust at the universities, once said: 'At Oxford and Cambridge the cooking is better than the curriculum. But there is no Chair of Cookery; it is learnt by apprenticeship in the kitchen'.

From birth a child lives in the workshop of language—his linguistic community. And since his primary concern is with content, this is where the teacher too must begin, if he is not to deprive himself of his chief ally, the children's interest in what is said to them or by them. If he can enlist this interest he can then lead them on to some attention to how it is said.

The mistake we can then make is to deceive ourselves that our interests and the children's are identical: that they can be as concerned as we are with form, or that we can be as concerned as they are with content. We are suggesting that here again it is only by clearly realizing that there is a difference of interests that a teacher can hope to keep his purposes clear and make them effective. He must aim at achieving his purposes for the children's future by helping them to achieve their immediate purposes now. While therefore his true concern is with form rather than matter, he must work with the principle that matter rather than form is the ostensible aim for the child.

The teacher who accepts this principle is then faced with a pressing practical question: 'Is the content to be wholly at the free will and choice of the children?'. It is doubtful whether any teacher can say an unqualified 'Yes' to this without some unease. He will know well enough that in fact he does exert some influence on choice; on what the children talk or write about, what they listen to or read, even what their private language is about. The practical question then is: 'Where should he come in?'.

3. Present values directed towards future needs

An answer enters as a logical corollary to Principles I and II taken together. If choice is to be influenced by the children's previous development and if priority is to be given to content rather than to language, then the themes must be determined by the children's present interests and needs.

So much as a logical conclusion. But what then becomes of the principle that we have taken as fundamental in all education—the twin regard for present values and future needs? Here again is a divergence of interests between teacher and pupil which poses an immediate practical problem in the classroom. The experience of many teachers indicates ways in which the problem can be met if not solved: that in the choice of themes present values can be compatible with future needs.

There are two or three basic considerations which can guide us here. First, we remember that a child's present interests and needs are not static; he is developing, moving forward. If we take too narrow a view of what is meant by allowing 'a child to live fully as a child', we are in danger of being too conservative in our estimate of what he is capable of, and so of imprisoning him in his own present. This conservatism may come from a mistaken fear of imposing

a restrictive discipline on him, perhaps even from a sentimentality which likes to feel that a child should be a child.
But in fact one of a child's chief present needs is the need
to grow up. A Peter Pan principle is a negation of education.

This leads to the recognition that in the cultivation of the
mother tongue, as in all education, we must always be
looking ahead, setting goals beyond a child's present
achievement. Goals may, of course, be too far ahead—this
is clear both in practical experience and from the systematic
study of processes of learning. Goals may be too far ahead
to be valid, not because they impose too heavy a burden,
but because they are too remote to be an incentive. In
linguistic education, how far ahead a goal can be, and yet
be a true goal—on this, research so far offers no guidance.
It remains something for the judgement of a teacher as a
result of experience.

A third consideration, particularly important in the
choice of what we bring to a child, is that between children's
and adult literature there is no clear boundary line, only a
broad borderland. On this the Plowden Committee, convinced as they are that a child should live fully as a child,
utter a salutary caution: 'Poetry written for adults, or at
least by those who are poets in their own right, is usually
to be preferred to children's verse'.[11] This has a wide
application throughout the choice of what we bring to a
child or allow him access to. It is a commonplace that some
of the books most enjoyed by children, and that we want
them to read, were not written for them. If the Committee
believe that a child should live fully as a child, they mean
also that a growing child has growing interests.

4. The uses of language must be as real as possible

There is sometimes a criticism of the school that it is
'artificial', in contrast to the realities of life at home and
in the street. But this difference there must be. A school is
an instrument of society, an agency specially designed to
shelter a child from the harsh realities of life, while preparing
him to meet them. It is an artefact, planned and ordered,

and therefore artificial by contrast with the rough-and-tumble of everyday life beyond its walls. As teachers we are faced with the question whether this artificiality may affect our tasks in the cultivation of children's language.

We have seen in Chapter 4 how it comes about that in school, language in communication and in private may lack the essential characters of its reality in everyday life. Whenever a child uses or responds to language in school, his teacher is inevitably there, playing a part, actual or potential. Even if he is not directly addressing his teacher, whenever a child speaks or writes, whether to others or for himself, he has his teacher in the corner of his eye. Or again, when he reads or listens, this is mostly under the choice and direction of his teacher, however delicately exerted. If we fail to see how all this is different from life outside the school—or, seeing it, say that it really does not matter—we may fail in what we are chiefly there for: to help the child to satisfy his real needs in language, now and in the future.

In the classroom, how real can language be? Going back once more to the basic uses of language, in communication and in private, we can say that for his linguistic development a child needs incentives for, and practice in, addressing a real audience, in being a real audience to others; and in making a real use of private language.

(i) *An audience for the child.* Can a teacher be a real audience for a child? In most reproductive speech and writing hardly at all. As we have seen, where a child is reproducing what he has learnt in class, the teacher is not someone to be informed or moved; he is, rather, one who provides the child with a yardstick for his own comprehension. In both incentive and practice this is a special kind of communication. The incentive for the child is to satisfy the teacher, to show that he can grasp and can communicate what has been communicated to him.

A teacher can only be a real audience when he is listening to something new to him—and the speaker believes this is so. In the classroom this can most naturally happen when

one child is speaking to the rest. Though classroom talks
were suggested by pioneers as long as fifty years ago, they
were slow in becoming general in schools; perhaps because
of the name Caldwell Cook coyly gave them—'Littleman
Lectures', perhaps even because the title of his book, *The
Play Way*, may have put off hard-headed, down-to-earth
teachers. Now they are common, as the Plowden Report
bears witness[12]; a change probably influenced, amongst
other things, by the children's familiarity with radio and
television. In these classroom talks more than anywhere else,
a teacher may be a real audience without pretence, and his
questions really intended to help him to understand what the
speaker is saying.

The main potential audience is, of course, the other
members of the class. But whether they become a real
audience, whether in fact classroom talks do anything to
train the children in productive speaking—this does not
happen of itself. Everything depends on how the talks
arise, how they are guided and carried on. This does not
mean, as the Plowden Report implies, that we have to wait
until the children are old enough to give formal talks. Even
in the infant school children's talk is certainly not limited
to a sentence at a time, and in the earlier years of the junior
school they can, of course, be encouraged to talk at length.
It is out of these informal beginnings that the more formal
speaking emerges. Here as always we can be in too much of
a hurry and try to get the children to do things for which
they are not yet ready. A teacher needs, more than anything
else, faith in the future. To be a teacher he must be an
optimist.

(*ii*) *An audience for writing*. What about a real audience
for a child's writing? One does not come across much
discussion of the possibilities of this, but it is obvious that
the need is no less great than for the spoken word. In
everyday adult life writing to others is hardly ever reproductive, in the sense of telling them what they already know.

In school, by contrast, reproductive writing is particularly
necessary. Not only does it let the teacher know how

successful he has been, it is also an excellent way of training the children to read or listen, to discriminate between the main theme and what is supplementary or irrelevant.

One important result of this is that even productive writing comes to be addressed to the teacher. This means that the children's experience of writing for a real audience is severely narrowed. Even when he asks them, encourages them, to write freely what they believe to be new to him, this very attempt may, by a paradox, seem no less artificial than the usual run of school writing. If most of the time a child is called upon to tell his teacher what he knows the teacher already knows, this comes to be the 'natural' thing in school. He may then feel that the object of 'free writing' is not really to set him free to say what he believes to be new to his reader, but only yet another way of 'teaching him English'.

Why not a real class audience for writing as well as for speech? The problems are in fact greater. Not only the general tradition and understanding that all writing in school is meant for the teacher; writing is still a formal, even laborious, business for children of junior school age—they don't usually write to each other. The initiative has to come from the teacher, but in such a way that a child feels that he is really writing to the others and they are really interested in what he has to say. Obviously this demands much of the skill and patience of the teacher, and is not easy. But something can be done. We look at detailed practical issues in the coming chapter.

(*iii*) *The child as listener or reader.* There is a complementary question not, perhaps, often asked: 'Is it necessary for the children to be a real audience for their teacher—in what comes directly from him, or indirectly through him, from books, radio and television? Is real participation by the children a necessary condition for communication with them in school?'

The practice of some teachers implies one answer to the question: that it doesn't matter whether the children are a real audience or not, that this is irrelevant to the achievement of our aims in the cultivation of their responses to what they hear or read. This answer is meant to express a tough, commonsense attitude, rejecting concessions to softness or sentimentality about children. It takes its stand on the unexceptionable ground that our task is to improve their ability to respond effectively to language in communication. It recognizes fully the need to widen and enrich their linguistic experience now, as well as to prepare them for richer and more discriminative listening and reading in their adult life. But it regards a search for their immediate and intrinsic participation as irrelevant, sometimes even inimical, to the achievement of these aims.

What is also implied though perhaps unsaid, is that here as throughout education, children are to be led rather than followed; that participation is to be a result instead of a condition of their linguistic education. Not their immediate interests but quite other incentives are to be involved: marks and other awards; the promise of qualifying for higher education; even compulsion—on the principle that what a child begins under compulsion he often continues of his own will. Further, moving from defence to attack, the argument continues that these incentives are much more powerful, stable and reliable than the shifting, uncertain and variable chances of children's primary participation as a real audience.

Much of this is not to be gainsaid. But it does not go far enough. It is not that the incentives and the means described are likely to be ineffective; the point is that they are not effective enough. They are what we may call extrinsic incentives, superimposed upon the task of understanding and appreciating what is read. Extrinsic incentives may help; but to set up habits of understanding and appreciation there must be intrinsic incentives—the wish and the intention to read.

A child can, of course, learn by imitation or under compulsion to do and say the right things in any situation. But, clearly, the test of our success in communicating with him is not what he says he ought to do, nor even what he says he does, but what he does. We can tell him and make him tell us what a book is about; he can learn to talk about language. But he must be engaged, caught up, if the combination of form and content is to be effective in communication. In fact, we can go to the other extreme and recognize that even an adult can respond to what is being communicated without being able to say very clearly what this is; he can respond to the combination of form and theme without being able to say how language and content are related to each other.

This suggests that we should begin with engagement and go on to scrutiny. Engagement means the desire to be in communication, the wish to comprehend, the willingness to surrender to the writer's imagination, to be moved by him; or where he demands a train of reasoning to pursue this with him. Then slowly and tentatively the rudiments of scrutiny emerge.

(iv) *The real use of private language.* We have seen the difficulty of cultivating private language in school; that while its value is that it is private, the teacher can help only by keeping an eye on it, so making it less private. The result of this may be that once again the child is writing for the teacher and so not getting real practice in writing for himself.

Special characteristics of private language

We have tried to show that since private and social language have different functions they have differences in form; that the standards of correctness demanded by the needs of social communication are irrelevant in private language and may even interfere with it; and that the very reasons for our insistence on correct grammar, spelling and punctuation in social communication are the grounds for tolerance and greater freedom in private language. These differences have practical implications in the classroom.

It is hardly necessary to point out that, without standard forms, communication would at the least be difficult, often chaotic, sometimes impossible. But not all the kinds of structure are equally important, and the differences offer guidance on what can be tolerated in private language.

In a linguistic community, it is accidence and syntax which obviously demand the closest uniformity, whether in speech or writing. These are the basic structures of a language. Compared with these, spelling and punctuation are no more than conventional aids to communication through the written word.

In spelling, rigorous standardization is clearly not essential for communication. If then we insist on standardized spelling, this is because it is convenient rather than essential. Except for wild idiosyncratic aberrations, considerable latitude does not impede communication. The present standardization of English spelling dates only from the mid-eighteenth century, yet it is possible to read letters of earlier times without undue difficulty, in spite of their sometimes bizarre inconsistencies of spelling. On the whole, the main justification for insisting on correct spelling is that it helps communication by politely saving the reader the bother of puzzling over unconventionally spelt words.

In punctuation, again, we have a number of conventions which help communication only if they are consistently used throughout a linguistic community; this is a principle which children can understand even in the junior school. They can see that if we use capitals and other marks of punctuation according to each one's taste and fancy, we are putting obstacles in the way of communication. The children can also see that legibility and neatness are aids to communication. Later on, in adolescence, they may also see that these conventions matter because of the impression they make on other people. This means that the grounds for correct grammar, punctuation and spelling and standards of neatness and legibility have no relevance when one is writing for oneself.

In all their writing children tend to be slowed down, even inhibited, if they have to give thought to such things as grammar, spelling, punctuation, legibility and neatness. But private language must be immediate, rapid, uninhibited; not

too laborious to bother about; something a child readily
uses, that he finds a help.

If in his private language a child is to be free of the
restrictions and conventions of social communication, this
is not merely an indulgent concession to his imperfect
command of writing. It is because this very freedom marks
off private from social language in adult life. It is essentially
individual and highly personal, sometimes so intimate as to
be unintelligible to others. At the extreme of privacy it may
be as personal as the secret code of a diary; but even a long
way short of this, most of us use abbreviations and symbols
in a scribble that nobody else could make out. It is just
because we can write it so speedily and heedlessly that it is
so much the more useful to us as private language. All that
we need is to be able to read it.

The permissive attitude to children's private language that
this suggests obviously invites a strong objection: that once
you allow them to be careless, once you tolerate their
mistakes in grammar, spelling or punctuation, you are
positively helping to produce bad habits. You are said to
be encouraging, even producing, habits that will work
against the standards necessary for successful social
communication.

The risk of this is clear; but to insist on the same correctness in private as in social language is to weaken if not
destroy the possibility of the real use of private language in
school. This is certainly what sometimes happens. Observations suggest that there must be many schools in which the
use of private written language is slight if not entirely
unknown. The problem to be faced is how to cultivate the
particular and different values of private and of social
language, without detriment to the development of either.

We need to establish a difference of attitude and approach.
In the early stages this will be no more than the children's
growing experience of what we allow, what we expect, what
we approve, in this private writing and in that social
writing. Out of these differences of practice, the children
gradually become aware of differences in standards, and

can be helped to see these more clearly, with benefit to both kinds of writing. As they get to know the reasons for tolerance in private language, it helps to sharpen their understanding that there cannot be the same permissiveness in social language; that the standards for this insisted on by the teacher, are not merely personal whims or things we have to do in school, but are necessities in social communication.

How far we are successful in promoting private language, so that the children spontaneously use it—this, here as elsewhere, will depend both on the strength of the incentives and the children's experience of the actual use of the language. The most powerful incentives will be a child's frequent realization that private language is really useful to him. Here, as much as anywhere, is the place for the teacher's discretion and skill. The fewer the number of isolated 'exercises' the better. Instead of tasks isolated from his needs at the moment, a child must have repeated experiences of the real use of private language. There is no need to invent occasions. In the course of daily life in school there is a wide diversity of opportunities, and needs, for private language. In the coming chapter we look at these and the relevant details of practice.

Notes

[1] Central Advisory Council for Education (England) (1967), ch. 16.
[2] Central Advisory Council for Education (England) (1967), p. 188.
[3] The idea that it is through the children that changes in language take place goes back at least as far as Jespersen (1922), chs. 9 and 10. It has recently been re-stated by McNeill (1966).
[4] Templin (1957), pp. 96, 119, 144.
[5] Page 31. For a fuller treatment, see Lewis (1963), p. 20.
[6] Lewis (1947), pp. 17 and 49-50, discusses this as it occurs in infancy and adult life. Lewis (1953), ch. 7, considers the possibility that resistance to literacy is a positive factor in backwardness in language.
[7] Central Advisory Council for Education (England) (1967), p. 222.
[8] Central Advisory Council for Education (England) (1967), p. 222.

[9] On p. 33, we have seen the uncertainties of the relations between directive language and action in infancy. The complexity of the relationships continues, certainly into childhood in the junior school, probably throughout life. For a summary of evidence, see Lewis (1963), pp. 180-6.

[10] Miller (1965).

[11] Central Advisory Council for Education (England) (1967), p. 217.

[12] Central Advisory Council for Education (England) (1967), p. 211. 'As they grow older and their self-assurance increases, occasions should be devised for them to talk, according to their capacity, to a group, to the class and at assembly'.

Chapter Six

Particular Problems of Practice

READING, writing, listening, speaking: nothing in school is more familiar or more commonplace. This book does not suggest new ways of doing these things, nor say as is sometimes said to the young teacher, 'Do this, not that'; but rather looks at what is being done and asks questions about it. In the cultivation of the mother tongue we have seen our aims determined by the children's present needs and by their future needs as adults. We have attempted to show that these aims may be translated into practice by four basic principles. We now come down to the things that go on in any junior school on any day, and ask how and in what conditions each may contribute to the linguistic development of the children and so to their general development.

Reading aloud, who reads to whom? Silent reading, what is its place and value in the junior school? Writing, social and private, when and how? Who speaks, on what and how? Who listens, to what and to whom?

To many people the answers will seem so obvious as to make the questions almost impertinent. All the same, let us ask them and bring into the open the implications of current practices. We look at the four streams of language development—reading, writing, speaking, listening—for what part is played in each of them by the three participants: the child, the teacher and the rest of the class.

Reading aloud

The Teacher to the Class

In any school on any day, teacher reads; the children listen, often without sight of the text; then the teacher asks questions about what he has read. We ask: What does he expect to give the children that they cannot get from their own silent reading? Why should the text be unseen by them? Why questions to follow?

What a teacher hopes to do is to improve the children's ability to read silently, since this, of course, is the essential skill needed by everyone in everyday life in a literate world. The teacher hopes through his reading to bring out what the writer intends—the theme, and the theme in relation to the language. He hopes to do this, not so much by talking about these things as by a sensitive interpretation, through emphasis, intonation and phrasing. It need hardly be said that few of us are capable of this without careful preparation.

Why with the text unseen by the children? A common answer is that this is a good way of getting them to attend and training them to listen. Now these results may or may not follow; whether they do depends not only on the teacher at this moment, how well he reads and what else he does, but also on the experience the children have had of being read to, through all the years since they came into the reception class in the infant school.

Certainly the children may be attending to the teacher; the question is whether they are attending to what he is reading. If this is boring or too difficult they may be watching him closely enough without taking in much of what he is reading. We have all found ourselves 'listening' to a preacher or lecturer in this way, our attention caught up by his appearance, dress or manner of speaking, but how much are we getting of what he is saying?

This suggests that there may be a positive value in letting the children see the text while they are being read to. An association can then be built up between the seen text and the expressiveness of the teacher's reading, so that his intonation, stress and pausing are incorporated into the text as seen, and may later influence the children's silent reading.

What is there to be said about the ordinary practice of asking the children questions after a reading? The obvious intention is not only to help the children to understand in retrospect what they have heard, but also, as they come to anticipate being questioned, to keep them alert during the reading. There is no doubt also that it has persisted in the practice of teachers because it is useful as a simple immediate test, to find out how far a reading has been effective.

It does not need a great deal of observation of what goes on in classrooms to see that this questioning may easily become a hindrance instead of a help to enjoyment and comprehension. The listening may degenerate into a routine of concentrating on the kind of topic on which the children have come to expect questions.

There is also a more fundamental point. To be asked questions after one has listened is something that hardly happens in everyday life outside the school. When children look at television or listen to radio, it is they who ask the questions. When we adults listen through these media or directly to a speaker from a platform, we certainly do not expect to be questioned. Most of us would resent it. Is it perhaps possible that children also resent it—or, at best, that they get so inured to school ways that they apathetically accept boredom?

On the other hand, after listening children certainly like to ask questions. Most of us know to our cost that outside school they don't need any encouragement.[1] Why not then in the classroom? There is the double justification that questioning is part of the normal development of children and that as adults we need to be able to ask the right questions in the right way. Training children to ask questions is at least as necessary for their future needs as training in answering.

But teachers who have recognized this and invited questions after a reading have found that this too may become a mechanical routine. Too often the children ask questions because they are expected to, not because they are really interested in the answers. They pick on unfamiliar words instead of the special meanings and effects of familiar words in unfamiliar contexts. Broader issues, such as the intention of the passage as a whole, or the sequence of thought, are left to go by the board.

Why not do what happens in everyday life—informal chat into which teacher and class drop their comments? A skilful teacher can, without asking questions, unobtrusively notice how effective his reading has been and do something to ensure that the important things have not been missed.

Let us add that it is just as well to have a reading sometimes without any follow-up at all. Even the most informal discussion if it becomes a routine can be a bore, damping down interest and lowering the temperature of enthusiasm.

One Child Reads Aloud

A seventeenth-century teacher returning today would find one practice in some schools familiar: 'reading round the class'. He would also soon discover that it is now frowned upon by colleges of education, inspectors of schools and many teachers, and that it is thought by the Plowden Committee to be a thing of the past.[2]

But it is by no means obsolete; and when we come upon the survival of a time-honoured practice though now under a cloud, it helps us to understand what we are about if we ask: Why was it favoured in the past and why no longer?

As to the past, in education in the classics, reading in turn made sure of the boys' pronunciation and their quantities. Apart from this, in the mother tongue it is the obvious way of teaching a child to read and testing him. And, of course, it is an easy way of keeping a class quiet and under the eye of the teacher.

Why then the objection? As in so much else in school, everything depends on why and how the thing is done. Reading round the class may make so little demand on the reader and the others as to be pretty useless to either. Too often the reader goes on in a slack and indifferent way, with the rest of the class hardly attending, doing little more than keeping an eye on the book so as to be ready to read in turn.

More positively, it can produce bad reading. It is painful to hear a child stumbling his way through a paragraph and completely ruining its effects for the other children.

In what conditions can there be a positive value in one child reading aloud in class? We first have to distinguish between those children who can read adequately and those who are backward in reading and need special attention. These the teacher must hear, but there is everything to be said against having this done in public. The teaching of a backward reader is most likely to be successful when it is private between him and his teacher.

Reading aloud by children who can read adequately can be useful if some precautions are taken. It needs careful preparation, often with the teacher's help, and to manage this in ordinary school conditions it becomes necessary to limit the number of readers on any one occasion. As few as three, perhaps; with the added advantage of avoiding the danger that besets everything we do in school, of becoming a boring routine. Given notice some days in advance, the reader would have time to choose and prepare, and perhaps get guidance from his teacher.

Freedom of choice offers a reader the opportunity of reading something new to the rest of the class. Nowadays there is likely to be a variety of books available in the classroom. The reader can be free to introduce a book that he himself likes. He has to think out how to make a chosen passage attractive to his listeners; and this is particularly where his teacher can help him. Some comment and discussion may follow, in the same sort of way as when the teacher has read to his class.

In these conditions, where a child has a real audience, the reading can make a contribution to the linguistic education of them all. If the audience are interested, they will listen, and may even be learning how to listen. For the reader himself its main value may be as much in the preparation as in the performance.

Silent reading in the junior school

It often seems to be implied that there is something special about silent reading, as though it were an accomplishment, to be added to the ability to read aloud, which is a necessity. In fact, it is the other way round. It is silent reading which is the natural aim and goal of the acquisition of the art of reading. In everyday adult life it is essential to be able to read silently; it is pleasant to be able to read well aloud.

In the ordinary way in school, children are in daily need of ability to read silently and so are constantly being trained in this skill. In the shopping games, for instance, that are carried over from the infant school, the children read advertisements, the names of things to be bought, and prices. In other games they read notes of instructions to be carried out. In early mathematics, silent reading plays a very large part; so-called 'problems' are tests of ability to read silently; and this has a positive value in the children's linguistic development that it is, by the criteria we have suggested earlier, a real situation. The silent reading is a means to an end, and the test of its effectiveness is pragmatic—the children see for themselves that careful reading has a practical value. They come to realize that in order to understand what the problem is, they have to read carefully; the task provides its own incentive.

In all these ways children get practice in silent reading; in addition, something can be done by way of special training. Children read a passage to themselves; this is followed by the same kind of discussion and questioning as happens after a reading aloud by the teacher. The Plowden Report strongly deprecates 'comprehension exercises on passages of literary quality', but does not say why they are objectionable.[3] It cannot be that children do not benefit from practice in understanding what they read. The loaded phrase 'comprehension *exercises*' is a clue to the objection. The Report is voicing the view of many teachers that harm may be done by some courses of English for schools where passages divorced from their context are set for study with questions to follow. A result is that children are led to look at the passage for those things that will help them to answer the questions, instead of really reading the passage.

As in so much else in schools, unenlightened work twists means into ends. The questions, instead of leading the children back to the context, become the aim of the exercise.

Does this mean that there is nothing to be said for the close study of 'a passage of literary quality?' The only—too obvious—answer is that this study should increase our understanding of its context: the paragraph or chapter of the book in which it appears. With this aim as a guide, there is a good deal to be said for the occasional reading of a book as a joint class activity, with the study of some passages. A variety of different kinds of reading can take their place quite naturally in this, under the kinds of precaution that we have indicated: reading aloud by the teacher, reading aloud by one child to the rest; silent reading by all members of the class, with discussion and questions to elucidate the context of a selected passage. The chosen extract may be a crucial stage in the narrative; it may throw special light upon characters in the story; it may help to provide the setting of the story. This then becomes training in real silent reading, leading a child to a recognition that special attention to a particular passage may enrich his understanding of its immediate and its broader contexts.

Writing, social and private

The teaching of English is notorious for being a hotchpotch of aims, intentions and practices. This is partly because the use of language includes so wide a field of behaviour, partly because it is so intimately familiar to us that it is difficult to see it objectively as a system of skills. In teaching someone to drive a car or to play tennis or to do arithmetic, we can remember how we ourselves learnt to do these things. But no one remembers how he learnt to speak and most of us have only the vaguest idea how we learnt to read and write.

The names we give to what we do in school may not matter very much. One change of name, however, which has been gaining ground does reflect a real difference of attitude and so of methods in the classroom. Instead of thinking of their work as the teaching of composition, many teachers now think of the development of the written word. This may be more cumbrous, but it has the advantage of reminding us that we are concerned to carry forward what has begun in the spoken word in earliest infancy. We help the children to carry forward in their writing the two main functions of the mother tongue: social communication and private language.

Social writing

To say that we are aiming at improving children's ability to communicate may seem too obvious until we notice the force of the word 'communicate'. This implies that when we are writing for others, most of the time this is not only 'self-expression': we are writing about something to somebody. For the teacher this means three problems of practice: the choice of theme, the audience, and the part the teacher himself has to play.

The Theme

There is nothing which owes more to the unobtrusive skill of a teacher than the manner in which the children's interest is engaged in what they are to write about. A young teacher today, imbued with a zeal for free expression by the children, may fail to recognize the possibilities, indeed the necessities, of other ways of stimulating the children to take on a theme. For, in addition to completely free choice, there is limited choice about a common theme, and also the set theme, one and the same for all the children.

No one can doubt that a free choice of theme is a powerful incentive for a child in getting him to want to say something to others as well as he can. But the teacher who, with the best will in the world, tries to give the children completely free choice, sooner or later finds that with some, if not all, he is defeating his own ends.

These are the children who, left to themselves, can think of nothing to write about. They will launch out only if given a fair start. In any case, a routine of spontaneity is not only logically absurd; in practice it stultifies itself by remaining a routine. It is not likely that every child will feel the urge to write about something every Thursday morning.

Above all, whatever the children are doing, in school the teacher is always there; and always, whether he realizes it or not, and however unobtrusively, a part of what is going on. Whether the class is working as a whole, or in groups or individually, there must be some system, some organization, in order that it is practicable for the teacher to make sure that every child is helped. Indeed it may be said that individuality, flexibility and freedom are most likely when they are aimed at within a framework of order and a regularity of practice.

The teacher comes in, sometimes to stimulate, sometimes to go further and suggest, sometimes to demand. For all children—even for those always ready to choose for themselves—there is something to be said for occasional limitation of choice. We may take a hint from a common practice in painting and drawing, where a limitation of choice becomes, almost paradoxically, a stimulus to free individual self-expression. A theme is suggested by the teacher and the children are encouraged to let their feelings and thoughts play about it. A wide variety of treatment often follows. But because there is a common theme there is an opportunity for lively and useful classwork both before writing begins and when it is finished.

There is also a place for a set theme, so long as there is a clear purpose. It is not enough, for instance, to ask simply for an accurate account of something that all have witnessed. This is a kind of writing different from the re-production by the child of what has previously been verbally presented to him and which, we have seen, certainly has its value.

No, here we are speaking of productive writing, communication with a real audience; and for this a child must feel that the writing has a purpose beyond being a test of him by the teacher. 'What did we see when we went to the fire-station last Wednesday? Let's see who can tell us exactly what happened and remind us of the most interesting things.' Now each child is not simply addressing the teacher. The judges of his accuracy and his liveliness are the rest of the class. Teachers find that they can begin this sort of thing quite early in the junior school, of course in a small way at first. If there is a class diary or log book of things done and the most accurate and lively pieces of writing are chosen for it, then the children do not have to be told that there should be a purpose in their writing—they experience it.

The Audience

Whether the theme is freely chosen or set or limited, if a child knows that he is writing for an audience, this will affect everything: the things he says, how he arranges them and the words he uses. It becomes important for a teacher to be clear about the different kinds of audience so that in one way or another the differences gradually become clear to the children also.

Nowadays, as the Plowden Report points out, things can be done in the junior school which thirty years ago seemed possible only in the secondary school.[4] A child's writing will gain much from his awareness that he is addressing a group of readers rather than a single person, his contemporaries rather than an adult. For this there can be a simple plan, now well-tried in many schools. What begins as a class diary may, as the children get older, become a class magazine. Once a month, for instance, every child is given the chance of choosing one piece of his recent work for inclusion in the magazine, which is no more than a collection of loose leaves held together in some convenient way.

Nor need there be any limitation on the kinds of writing; the themes may be freely chosen, or limited or set; in verse or prose; narrative, description or exposition. In a class of thirty to forty children there may be circulating at any one time three gazettes of about a dozen pieces each. When every child has read at least one gazette, there may be class discussion; or, as we move up through the school, the gazettes may have a blank sheet after each piece of writing, for signed comments by readers. The sheets go back with the writings to the authors.

This is more likely to be successful at the top of the school if it is begun in the simplest way, in the first year or two. As soon as a class diary gets under way, discussions on what to include, and comments on what is included, begin. As time goes on, these comments may sometimes be written down privately—perhaps no more than single words —before class discussion. Over the years the laconic comments expand.

One important result is that it gets rid of the feeling that every piece of writing is an exercise. Of course there is a place for exercises in writing, but these should be felt to be different from the real job of addressing someone. If writing is a system of skills, there is a good analogy with a craft such as woodwork. Special exercises are useful, even necessary; but every now and then a child *makes* something.

Not the least value of the audience that a class magazine provides is that this gets over the problem of the 'fair copy' in a rational way. The problem, as the Plowden Report suggests,[5] is that teachers who wish to free their children from the binding tyranny of a fair copy of every piece of writing, fear that to accept rough scribbles may encourage carelessness. But when a child chooses a piece of work for inclusion in a class gazette, he has an incentive and a natural reason for presenting it as well as possible. Other 'unpublished' work, the teacher may be willing to accept at a lower level of presentation, while yet expecting some care. The criterion must always be how far a child's attempts at the graces of presentation—spelling, punctuation, legibility—may inhibit real communication.

There remains another kind of audience—the person to whom we write a letter. Now, in contrast to the kinds of audience we have been describing, it is not natural for a child in the classroom to write a letter to his teacher or to a group of other children. Yet there is no need to invent occasions for imaginary letters: the ordinary day's work offers opportunities enough; in connection with classroom projects and school visits, letters of inquiry and letters of thanks. By a combination of co-operation and competition the letter goes out as a joint product of the whole class. Different, again, is the letter sent to an absent member of the class, ill at home or in hospital. The existence in these cases of a real situation will do much to influence the choice of language and the general manner of writing.

If we are insisting here on the importance of an audience in all social writing, it is because this is in line with what we know of the early development of language and what we can see of writing in adult life. From his earliest cries in infancy—apart from his private language—a child is always addressing his utterance to someone in particular. And this remains true in adult life. If therefore much of a child's writing is without a clear destination, we are not giving him the kind of practice he needs; we are not continuing his linguistic development towards his needs in his adult life.

The Teacher

The teacher enters the business of writing at several different points: at the choice of theme, the provision of an audience, help and guidance in the techniques of writing, correction and improvement.

(a) *Choice of theme.* The teacher can ensure that when completely free choice is offered it should not be felt as compulsory, that the child should not feel that he is being forced to choose for himself. There should always be alternatives; while some of the class are choosing freely others are expecting guidance or even a set theme. Wherever the teacher enters at all, his difficulty is to keep a balance between withholding himself and having too much influence. Attempting to stimulate the children and suggest fruitful possibilities, he may be leading them much more powerfully than he realizes.

Where the theme is set to the whole class, both he and they can play a larger part in discussion. When all, for instance, have witnessed the event they are about to record, discussion opens the eyes of some to what others have observed and reminds some of what others remember. The teacher himself can contribute to this as a member of the group; he also has the special function of seeing that the initiative of some children is not weakened by easy reliance on others. Getting them all to make a list of what they remember provides a natural opportunity for the use of private language.

(b) *Audience*. Whether the theme is freely chosen, or limited, or set, the teacher can do a very great deal in bringing the child to be clear about whom he is addressing. It need hardly be said that this is best done not by constantly talking about it but rather by the occasional judicious word: that now a child is writing for the teacher, now writing for a wider audience, now writing a letter to a particular person.

(c) *Guidance in writing*. One of the main problems for a teacher is to give the children guidance without obtruding on them the premature discussion of techniques. This in fact is a problem in the school development of skills in general—in handwork, in drawing and painting, in games. All these are acquired by a combination of imitation and exploration; and this, as we have tried to show, is particularly true of linguistic skills.

But there is one important fact of skill in writing that marks it off from any other skills. This is, that while a child is still in the earliest and most rudimentary stages of writing, he is already well advanced in his mastery of language.

Writing is the enlargement of this mastery—from sounds in the air to marks on paper. Because some children find the transition difficult, some teachers have sought a way out by breaking down the craft of writing into its simplest components and then building these up step by step. A logical progress is planned. The children write sentences, then combine these into paragraphs and these again into stories.

What's wrong with this? Many people today feel that it is wrong. In the Plowden Report, for instance, the whole treatment of writing breathes a spirit of freedom for the child, for him to take the plunge, without any preliminary exercises at the side of the pool. Here we have to ask: What could be wrong with the method of analysis and synthesis that we have described?

What is wrong is the fallacy of confusing two different kinds of analysis; the mistake of supposing that if we analyse the usages of the mother tongue as it is, we shall lay bare the factors of its development in children. A study of the mother tongue is useful, indeed essential, if we are to be clear about the goals towards which we are directing our work with the children; but how to do this can only be found by studying the children before, in and out of school. The linguists who follow Chomsky in the analytic and synthetic study of language warn us against identifying this with the study of the practice of language.[6]

Certainly everything we have said here about linguistic development and the principles of cultivating the mother tongue in school leads to the conclusion that the only sound approach to writing is not to treat the children as though they were literally 'infants', that is, 'without speech'; but that, recognizing their considerable command of language, to furnish them as quickly as possible with the rudimentary techniques that will enable them to speak on paper—and then let them speak freely.

It is the realization of this, as much as anything else, that has brought about what the Plowden Report terms 'the most dramatic of all the revolutions in English teaching'; that is, encouraging 'free, fluent and copious writing', which sometimes goes to the extreme of believing 'there is virtue in sheer volume, irrespective of what is said'.[7]

The danger is well known to teachers: writing that is too fluent, too copious, badly ordered, ill-directed. Given freedom, the children need guidance. The teacher is faced with the problem of correcting errors as well as helping the children to improve their ability to use language.

(d) *Correction and improvement.* It is obvious that correction of itself does not necessarily bring improvement, yet it is not too much to say that the actual practice of some teachers—'marking the children's work', 'correcting their compositions'—assumes that it does. Here we have to distinguish between these two and ask what is the place of each in the guidance that a teacher can give.

What has research to tell us? The methods and the effects of correction and improvement have been studied in innumerable investigations in other fields. We are in the realm of the psychology of learning with its welter of hypotheses, experiments and controversies. But research has little or nothing to offer us here. It is evident to some linguists today that whatever may have been achieved in the study of non-verbal learning cannot simply be applied to the acquisition of language.[8] Specific research is still in its infancy. We have to rely on ordinary observation of children and everyday classroom practice.

By correction we mean bringing a child's language into conformity with current usage; by improvement we mean enhancing the effectiveness of his language functionally, both as a means of communication and in its private use. In correcting children's writing we attempt to bring it into line with accepted usage; to ensure as far as we can that the children use the current forms—spelling, accidence, syntax—and use them with the meanings they have in educated current language. In aiming at this, as we have suggested earlier, a good deal of tolerance is necessary; not only because, as Gowers has pointed out, the current language allows this, but because it is extremely important not to arouse the children's resistance to attempts to change their customary language. As a result, at any rate in the earlier years in the junior school, we must be willing to accept some forms and some semantic usages that we ourselves may not like.

What we see so often in everyday life is that correction by a teacher is efficient if it is not only of, but also by, the learner. Children must participate as fully as possible in their own correction. Here we come to a problem that particularly troubles some teachers. Obviously it is not enough to show a child where he is wrong; not enough, even, to tell him what is right. Unless his effort and intention are involved, there is likely to be a low level of incentive and so of effective learning.

Teachers try to get over this difficulty by requiring the children to find the correct forms and usages for themselves; for instance, from a dictionary. But this is clearly of very limited application; least for the errors that matter most— that is, for the commonest, most familiar words. For example, confusion between *as, has; is, his; their, there;* mistakes such as *I buyed; I taked;* in none of these will the dictionary help. The teacher has no option but to give the correct form or meaning. Only then can the child be actively involved, by having to practise the correct form, perhaps by rewriting the sentences in which the errors have occurred.

This brings us to the vexed question of the amount of correction. Discussions with teachers show that many are uneasy about leaving any errors uncorrected. This is plain conscientiousness, coupled with a fear of being too indulgent and a fear that an uncorrected error may become more firmly established.

Many of the teachers are, however, uneasy because they see that it is the least able children who are given the most correction to do. The very children who most need help benefit least. The teacher's conscientiousness defeats itself.

We know from our own experiences as learners that too much correction can be worse than useless. In learning to drive a car or to ski, we should think an instructor inefficient who said: 'Yes, you're doing nicely, but there are fourteen different mistakes you've made. They are . . .' We should expect him to select and help us with three or four of our most important mistakes before we were told about any more.

Can we have this kind of selection in the correction of children's writing? It may require courage, especially in going through a child's work privately with him. When common errors are dealt with in class, selection is no less necessary. For this kind of public discussion to be useful, the way in which each error is to be treated must be prepared beforehand. It is doubtful whether the not unknown practice of casual chat about children's work is worth the time spent on it.

Time must be given for the children to follow up the corrections indicated by the teacher. This might be when the ablest children are going on with their writing; but it is obviously important that the less able children should not feel that they are kept grinding away at dull routine, while other children are enjoying the interesting and lively job of fresh writing. This brings in another reason for limiting the number of corrections to be dealt with.

Some teachers who accept all this nevertheless feel that they must indicate every error, without however requiring all of them to be corrected. This feeble compromise would not matter if it hadn't the disconcerting and depressing effect of a page of writing scored line after line with red ink. It may require courage, but there is everything to be said for indicating only those errors that have to be dealt with.

The difference between correcting a child's errors and improving his ability in writing is very much the same as the old antithesis between instruction and education. In correcting a child we are instructing him, telling him what is the current, approved usage. We are requiring him to conform to conventions—of grammar, spelling and punctuation, for which we can sometimes give him rules. These conventions he has to take from us; what we tell him is correct we expect him to accept—though, as we have said, we should allow a certain measure of flexibility and tolerance.

But when we come to the improvement of his writing, helping to make his communication more effective, our relationship with him is different. Now we are educating him; developing an ability he already has—the ability to communicate, to evoke thought and feeling in another person. This is not to be done by keeping to a set of rules. We learn how to communicate by experience; by realizing how others achieve, or fail to achieve, communication with us; by observing as well as we can the responses of others to ourselves.[9]

What a teacher can do is to help children to realize these things for themselves, in their reading and their writing. We have seen the possibilities of the class conversations that may follow on something read; the children can be invited now and then to think about a sentence or two and ask, with the teacher, what the writer is trying to say and how well he is managing to say it. It is, however, easy to forget that writers of books are craftsmen a very long way beyond any child's skill. What most children benefit most from is the study of what their contemporaries do.

When children have the opportunity of reading each other's work the teacher still has an essential function. Reading the pieces of writing for himself, he can make up his mind which points he will lead the class to discuss. This, as we have said, may begin in a small way in the earlier years of the junior school. However informal or brief the discussion, preparation by the teacher can make all the difference. What is this boy telling us? Would a change of word—or phrase or sentence—help him to do this better? This is not, as some courses of English seem to suggest, that some words or phrases are better, absolutely, and that children have to learn them. Nor is there any particular merit in variety. The question always is: What is the fitness of this word or phrase in its context; how well does it enable the writer to express what he is trying to say.

It is not even that the teacher is the authority, the repository of better writing. It is, rather, that through him the classroom with its audience becomes a workshop where the critics learn at least as much as the writers. And these critics have the advantage over professional critics in adult life that they are so much the better able to learn because they themselves have been trying to do the same thing or something like it.

If there has been a limited choice of theme, there can be useful comparisons of varieties of points of view and of treatment. If there has been a single set theme, different attempts give the teacher an excellent opportunity of comparing their relative effectiveness. All know what has been written about; which of these two attempts does it more clearly, accurately, vividly? How?

Where there has been completely free choice, a different procedure becomes necessary. Here, one thing may be chosen from a child's work to illustrate a particular point of technique in communication. In discussion, alternatives may be suggested and compared with what the writer himself has said. All this can be done in an informal way so that even at the top of the school it is felt, not as yet another routine, but rather as a natural part of the business of learning to write.

Private writing

At the end of Chapter 5 we indicated the nature, functions and forms of private language. Here we need do no more than suggest ways in which the general principles can be put into practice in private writing in school. To make private writing a real use of language, so that the children are convinced of its value and even of its necessity, the teacher should take advantage of the opportunities offered in the everyday course of things rather than invent occasions for its introduction.

First, private writing can be a very good way in which a child prepares himself for a piece of written communication. Children, like adults, differ in the kind of preparation they find useful. Some jot down ideas in any order they come. Others like to sketch out a plan for the whole piece of writing, perhaps no more than three or four headings— sometimes the titles of three or four pictures that could tell the story. Others, again, may feel disposed to write down no more than the title of the whole thing, adding perhaps notes on one or two salient points.

While none of this private preparation need be meant for the eye of the teacher, his intervention can be useful, and felt to be useful, if he is tentative and unobtrusive and suggests rather than insists. He can mention other kinds of preparation than those that a child is inclined to use. He can indicate that instead of the explicit and full language of social writing, a shortened form of expression is sufficient, even essential, if private writing is not to become too laborious to be of practical value.

In preparation for discussion, private writing also has an important place. We have seen that in the class or group discussion which may precede writing within a limited choice of theme or on a set theme, there is always the possibility of demanding too little initiative of the less able and less energetic members. One way of obviating this is to arrange that sometimes, for a few minutes before a discussion, each child is expected to do a little thinking on paper. And while this is going on, the teacher can be having a word with individual children, by way of guiding them to the most profitable use of this private preparation.

In very much the same way, private preparation may be used for the discussions that precede other joint activities; for instance, a letter from the whole class, planning a presentation to somebody, arranging the dramatization of a story, making the preliminary plans for a school journey or a visit. Any of these occasions offers an opportunity for each child to put down his thoughts privately before the discussion begins. It need hardly be said that this should not be allowed to harden into a formalized routine, so that every discussion is solemnly preceded by a period of private writing. It is, rather, that this should be done often enough to become a natural way of leading up to discussion. We have a picture of the classroom on these lines: pencil or ball-point ready to hand, each child may now and then jot down something in his 'rough' book.

Speaking and listening

There remains one more use of a child's private writing—preparation for a talk to the rest of the class. If this more formal speech is to take its place in a child's linguistic education it must, no less than every other use of language, be related to his present as well as to his future needs. What we can do becomes clearer if we compare the conditions likely to make his speaking effective with those necessary for effective writing; how far these are alike, how far different.

What is common to both writing and speaking is the main aim: the ability to communicate with others. Everything else must be subordinate to this main aim, nothing must conflict with it. Such things as grammatical correctness, spelling and legibility in writing have their parallels in the spoken medium—pronunciation, enunciation, intonation, stress, pausing, speed—all the characteristics which are usually attended to in speech training. In the spoken word as in writing there is the same problem for the teacher; to bear in mind that these are all features of the *structures* of language; that they are only important as they help the functions of language.

The difficulties of making speech training a means to the development of spoken communication are well known. Often enough it fails to convince the children that it is in any way relevant to the effectiveness of speaking. Because it makes them self-conscious, it may inhibit instead of promoting communication. Yet speech training is attractive to some teachers because it lends itself to systematic treatment which can—almost—be reduced to a set of rules. A course of exercises can be planned in advance and taken at regular intervals. There will perhaps be noticeable improvements in speech—in pronunciation, intonation, enunciation and the rest. But to achieve the only justifiable intention of all this—to promote and facilitate spoken communication—is infinitely more difficult. For this, a teacher needs initiative and the ability to adapt himself to conditions as they arise. He can, however, be guided by keeping in mind the basic necessities in all communication, whether spoken or written: choice of theme, preparation and the presence of a real audience.

(a) *Choice of Theme*

If there is to be real communication between a speaker and his listeners, the range of choice of theme becomes much more limited than for writing. In everyday life, speaking at length is likely to be re-creative rather than creative. We give an account of events that have occurred or we explain a process or, possibly, pursue a line of argument. The possibilities of imaginative, creative expression that we encourage in children's writing hardly exist when they are speaking at length.

Other differences between speaking and writing also have a bearing on the choice of theme. When a child is not directly addressing his teacher, or writing a letter, what he writes has only a potential audience in mind; but when he speaks his audience is actual, immediately there. There must be engagement of speaker and audience if there is to be real communication.

All this means that the choice of theme is decided by what the child himself is interested to talk about and which he has reason to believe his audience will be interested to hear about. Choice has to be freer than in writing. Topics set by the teacher or even grouped about a set theme are likely to produce no more than school exercises in speaking instead of real communication.

A teacher who likes to plan all his work will find it difficult, if not impossible, to fit formal speaking, 'lecturettes', into a planned programme, in which the members of the class appear in turn, in a predetermined order. The succession of talks has to be much more casual and incidental. The teacher has to use his knowledge of his pupils, and no little skill, in choosing those whom he can ask or stimulate to speak. If as a result some remain excluded, this is surely better than insisting upon what must be a pretence at communication by an unconcerned or even unwilling child. A teacher with his wits about him will find opportunities for getting children even of this kind to speak sometimes—if not formally or at length. And every child can be expected to be an active listener, to participate as a member of an audience.

(b) *Preparation*

We begin with the basic principle that the intention of preparation is not to write out at length what is to be read aloud, but to make a plan for speaking. This is by no means easy even for adults; with children, not to be had simply for the asking; it is something that has to be learnt. If ability to speak at length is accepted as one of the aims of linguistic education, then training in planning to speak becomes an essential element in this.

In the junior school, preparation for public speaking offers good opportunities for the development of private writing. The preparation cannot be done in public, cannot be a classroom project, as preparation for a good deal of writing can well be; but the child still needs the help of his teacher. Preparation for speaking becomes a combination of the child's initiative and his teacher's guidance.

The main problem of this preparation, and the value of its challenge to the child, is the difficulty of thinking ahead, of anticipating what one is going to say without setting it down in full. Learning how to do this is a slow process, and as teachers we have to recognize that it owes much to experience and is therefore likely to be only rudimentary while the child is still with us in the junior school. To expect, still more to insist on, an ordered treatment is likely to stifle initiative and to stultify the development of uninhibited real communication in speaking.

Once, then, the theme has been chosen, the child should be free to put down his ideas on paper as they occur to him. They may, if he is of that turn of mind, fall into a well-ordered sequence; more often this is where the teacher's help and guidance will be needed. Time for a private word with the child can be found while the rest of the class are busy writing, or correcting past work.

The result of the child's preparation under the guidance of his teacher should be a set of brief notes, headings, from which he will speak. It is not too much to say that in this preparatory work, the thought that it demands of the child can be as valuable a part of his linguistic education as the actual business of speaking.

(c) *A Listening Audience*

Most important of all in the cultivation of spoken communication is the presence of a real audience. More even than in writing it directly affects the task of the speaker; and in a number of ways. First of all, the audience in front of him puts him at once into a situation of real communication. It is to these people that he must speak; and if this sense of direction, this special relationship of confrontation and engagement, does not immediately spring from the fact that he is speaking to them, he can soon be helped to realize it, much more readily than in writing.

Secondly, by the manner in which his listeners listen, they exercise a continued effect on him, silently demanding from him those qualities of speaking that make for good communication. Here again, if he is at first oblivious of this come-back from his audience, he can without much difficulty be made aware of it.

Finally the response from the audience can be helpful to him and to themselves when it has become vocal and explicit after he has finished speaking. They ask questions and make comments. Later, perhaps not until the secondary stage of their education, some of the comments will begin to take the form of critical judgements of the effectiveness of his speaking as communication.

Indeed the most important factor in the development of spoken communication is not the personal intervention of the teacher. By keeping in the background during and after a talk by one of the class, he can discreetly bring the responses of the listeners to bear upon the speaker.

In this way, public speaking by one member of a class becomes a way of training all in the art of listening. Teachers are sometimes doubtful about the value of classroom lectures; they say: One child is working; what are the rest of the class doing?

The rest of the class may be doing very little; but they could be doing a great deal, for themselves and the speaker. They can be brought to listen actively—and this depends as much on the teacher's attitude and what he expects, as on the speaker. The children's questions afterwards will tell the speaker, and themselves, how well they have understood him; how well he has arranged what he is trying to say; how suitable and effective his choice of words has been.

What we are saying here about the spoken word is one more example of what we have had to notice throughout our thinking about the linguistic education of children. Study and investigation today lead us to see that the development of language is a highly complicated series of processes, about which we know little enough, but in which a teacher can certainly play a part. He will best be able to help if he is clear about his aims for the children, both now and in their future; if he keeps in mind their previous development as well as the structures and functions of the mother tongue in adult life; if he recognizes that there are basic principles of practice, and is able to carry them out with skill tempered with commonsense.

Notes

[1] There have been many investigations into children's questions. The study by Nathan Isaacs, appended to his wife's book (Susan Isaacs, *Intellectual Growth in Young Children*, 1930) has never been superseded. Other studies are by McCarthy (1954), and Lewis (1951), ch. 14.

[2] Central Advisory Council for Education (England) (1967), p. 216.

[3] Central Advisory Council for Education (England) (1967), p. 216.

[4] Central Advisory Council for Education (England) (1967), p. 218.

[5] Central Advisory Council for Education (England) (1967), p. 221.

[6] Miller and McKean (1964). 'A description of a language and a description of actual performances by language users must be kept distinct . . . Of course, a language user's performance reflects his tacit knowledge of the language, but the actual procedures whereby he attempts to comply with the rules that he knows are little understood. Indeed, the psychological study of these processes has scarcely begun'.

[7] Central Advisory Council for Education (England) (1967), pp. 218-9.

[8] Miller (1965) warns us: 'Human language is a subtle and complex thing; there are many aspects that, if not actually unique, are at least highly distinctive of our species, and whose nature could scarcely be suspected, much less extrapolated, from the analysis of non-verbal behaviour'.

[9] The processes of feedback have become an important part of the psychology of learning and of communication. See, for instance, Lunzer and Morris (1968), vol. 2, pp. 112-4 and 393-6, 'cybernetics'.

References

ALEXANDER, S. (1933). *Beauty and Other Forms of Value*. London: Macmillan.

BELLUGI, U. and BROWN, R. W. eds. (1964). 'The acquisition of language', *Monogr. Soc. Res. Child Developm.*, vol. 29, no. 1 (whole no.), pp. 1-192.

BERNSTEIN, B. (1958). 'Some sociological determinants of perception: an inquiry into sub-cultural differences', *Brit. J. Sociol.*, vol. IX, no. 2, pp. 159-74.

BERNSTEIN, B. (1960). 'Language and social class', *Brit. J. Sociol.*, vol. XI, no. 3, pp. 271-6.

BERNSTEIN, B. (1964). 'Social class, speech systems and psychotherapy', *Brit. J. Sociol.*, vol. XV, no. 1, pp. 54-64.

BOARD OF EDUCATION: SECONDARY SCHOOL EXAMINATIONS COUNCIL: SPECIAL COMMITTEE. (1943). *Curriculum and Examinations in Secondary Schools*. (Norwood Report). London: HM Stationery Office.

BRINSLEY, J. (1612). *Ludus Literarius*. London.

BURT, C. (1937). *The Backward Child*. (Rev. ed. 1961). London: University of London Press.

CARMICHAEL, L. ed. (1954). *Manual of Child Psychology*. New York: Wiley.

CENTRAL ADVISORY COUNCIL FOR EDUCATION (ENGLAND). (1967). *Children and their Primary Schools*. (Plowden Report). London: HM Stationery Office.

CHOMSKY, N. (1959). 'Review of *Verbal Behaviour* by Skinner', *Language*, vol. XXXV, pp. 26-58. (also In: JAKOBOVITS, L. A. AND MIRON, M. S. eds.)

CHOMSKY, N. (1962). *Syntactic Structures*. The Hague: Mouton.

CHOMSKY, N. (1964). 'Formal discussion', *Monogr. Soc. Res. Child Developm.*, vol. 29, no. 1, pp. 35-9.

COOK, H. C. (1915). *The Play Way*. London: Heinemann.

DARWIN, C. (1929). *Autobiography*. London: Watts.

ELIOT, T. S. (1928). *The Sacred Wood*. (2nd ed.) London:Methuen.

FREUD, S. (1927). *The Ego and the Id*. London: Hogarth Press.

FURTH, H. G. (1966). *Thinking without Language*. London: Collier-Macmillan.

GOWERS, E. (1962). *The Complete 'Plain Words'*. London: Penguin.

HOUSMAN, A. E. (1933). *The Name and Nature of Poetry*. Cambridge: Cambridge University Press.

JAKOBOVITS, L. A. and MIRON, M. S. eds. (1967). *Readings in the Psychology of Language*. Englewood Cliffs, N.J. Prentice-Hall.

JESPERSEN, O. (1922). *Language*. London: Allen & Unwin.

LAWTON, D. (1968). *Social Class, Language and Education*. London: Routledge & Kegan Paul.

†LENNEBERG, E. H. (1964a). 'A biological perspective of language'. In: Lenneberg, E. H. ed. *New Directions in the Study of Language*. Cambridge, Mass. MIT Press.

LENNEBERG, E. H. (1964b). 'Speech as a motor skill with special reference to nonaphasic disorders', *Monogr. Soc. Res. Child Developm.*, vol. 29, no. 1, pp. 115-27.

LEWIS, M. M. (1947). *Language in Society*. London: Nelson.

LEWIS, M. M. (1951). *Infant Speech*. (2nd ed.) London: Routledge & Kegan Paul.

LEWIS, M. M. (1953). *The Importance of Illiteracy*. London: Harrap.

LEWIS, M. M. (1963). *Language, Thought and Personality in Infancy and Childhood*. London: Harrap.

LEWIS, M. M. (1968). *Language and Personality in Deaf Children*. Slough: NFER.

LLOYD-JAMES, A. (1935). *The Broadcast Word*. London: Kegan Paul.

LUNZER, E. A. and MORRIS, J. F. eds. (1968). *Development in Human Learning*. London: Staples Press.

†LURIA, A. R. (1959). 'The directive function of speech in development and dissolution, parts I and II', *Word*, vol. 15, pp. 341-52, 453-64.

LURIA, A. R. (1961). 'The role of speech in the regulation of normal and abnormal behaviour'. In: SIMON, B. and SIMON, J. *Educational Psychology in the USSR*. London: Routledge & Kegan Paul.

MCCARTHY, D. (1954). 'Language development in children'. In: CARMICHAEL, L. ed. *Manual of Child Psychology*. New York: Wiley; pp. 492-631.

MCLUHAN, H. M. (1964). *Understanding Media*. New York: McGraw-Hill.

†MCNEILL, D. (1966). 'The creation of language', *Discovery*, vol. 27, no. 7, pp. 34-8.

MALINOWSKI, B. (1923). 'The problem of meaning in primitive languages'. In: OGDEN, C. K. and RICHARDS, I. A. *The Meaning of Meaning*. London: Routledge.

MEAD, G. H. (1934). *Mind, Self and Society*. Chicago: University of Chicago Press.

MEDAWAR, P. B. (1967). *The Art of the Soluble*. London: Methuen.

†MILLER, G. A. (1965). 'Some preliminaries to psycholinguistics', *Amer. Psychologist*, vol. 20, pp. 15-20.

†MILLER, G. A. and MCKEAN, K. O. (1964). 'A chronometric study of some relations between sentences', *Quart. J. Exper. Psychol.*, vol. 16, pp. 297-308.

†Also in: OLDFIELD, R. C. and MARSHALL, J. C. eds. (1968). *Language*. Harmondsworth: Penguin.

OGDEN, C. K. and RICHARDS, I. A. (1949). *The Meaning of Meaning.* (10th ed.) London: Routledge & Kegan Paul.

OLDFIELD, R. C. and MARSHALL, J. C. eds. (1968). *Language.* Harmondsworth: Penguin.

OPIE, I. and OPIE, P. (1959). *The Lore and Language of Schoolchildren.* London: Oxford University Press.

OSGOOD, C. E. and MIRON, M. S. eds. (1963). *Approaches to the Study of Aphasia.* Urbana, Ill. University of Illinois Press.

PIAGET, J. (1923). *Le Langage et la Pensée chez l'Enfant.* Paris: Delachaux et Niestlé.

PIAGET, J. (1953). *Logic and Psychology.* Manchester: Manchester University Press.

PINK, M. A. (1946). 'The teaching of prose composition'. In: PINTO, V. DE S. ed. *The Teaching of English in Schools.* London: Macmillan; pp. 84-99.

PINTO, V. DE S. ed. (1946). *The Teaching of English in Schools.* London: Macmillan.

RUSHTON, J. (1966). 'The relationship between personality characteristics and scholastic success in eleven-year-old children', *Brit. J. Educ. Psychol.*, vol. XXXVI, pt. 2, pp. 178-84.

RUSSELL, B. (1921). *The Analysis of Mind.* London: Allen & Unwin.

SAMPSON, O. (1964). 'Written composition at ten years as an aspect of linguistic development', *Brit. J. Educ. Psychol.*, vol. XXXIV, pp. 143-50.

SKINNER, B. F. (1957). *Verbal Behaviour.* London: Methuen.

SPREEN, O. (1965). 'Language functions in mental retardation', *Amer. J. Ment. Deficiency*, 69, pp. 482-94.

STRANG, B. M. H. (1962). *Modern English Structure.* London: Edward Arnold.

TEMPLIN, M. C. (1957). *Certain Language Skills in Children.* Minneapolis: University of Minnesota Press.

TOLSTOY, L. N. (1929). *What is Art?* and *Essays on Art.* London: Oxford University Press.

TOLSTOY, L. N. (1957). *War and Peace.* Harmondsworth: Penguin.

VIGOTSKY, L. S. (1962). *Thought and Language.* New York: Wiley.

WEIR, R. H. (1963). *Language in the Crib.* The Hague: Mouton.

Index